The Real Estate Developer's Handbook

Revised 2nd Edition

How to Set Up, Operate, and Manage a Financially Successful Small Real Estate Development Firm

By Tanya Davis

The Real Estate Developer's Handbook: How to Set Up, Operate, and Manage a Financially Successful Small Real Estate Development Firm Revised 2nd Edition

Copyright © 2016 Atlantic Publishing Group, Inc.
1405 SW 6th Avenue • Ocala, Florida 34471 • Phone 800-814-1132 • Fax 352-622-1875
Web site: www.atlantic-pub.com • E-mail: sales@atlantic-pub.com
SAN Number: 268-1250

Library of Congress Cataloging-in-Publication Data

Names: Davis, Tanya R., 1962- author.
Title: The real estate developer's handbook : how to set up, operate, and
   manage a financially successful small real estate development firm / by
   Tanya Davis.
Description: Revised 2nd edition. | Ocala : Atlantic Publishing Group, 2016.
   | Revised edition of the author's The real estate developer's handbook,
   2007. | Includes bibliographical references and index.
Identifiers: LCCN 2015041508 (print) | LCCN 2015045947 (ebook) | ISBN
   9781601389480 (alk. paper) | ISBN 1601389485 (alk. paper) | ISBN
   9781601389619 ()
Subjects: LCSH: Real estate developers--United States--Handbooks, manuals,
   etc. | Real estate developers--Handbooks, manuals, etc. | Real estate
   development--United States--Handbooks, manuals, etc. | Real estate
   development--Handbooks, manuals, etc.
Classification: LCC HD255 .D38 2016 (print) | LCC HD255 (ebook) | DDC
   333.33068--dc23
LC record available at http://lccn.loc.gov/2015041508

Printed in the United States

Printed on Recycled Paper

Reduce. Reuse. RECYCLE.

A decade ago, Atlantic Publishing signed the Green Press Initiative. These guidelines promote environmentally friendly practices, such as using recycled stock and vegetable-based inks, avoiding waste, choosing energy-efficient resources, and promoting a no-pulping policy. We now use 100-percent recycled stock on all our books. The results: in one year, switching to post-consumer recycled stock saved 24 mature trees, 5,000 gallons of water, the equivalent of the total energy used for one home in a year, and the equivalent of the greenhouse gases from one car driven for a year.

Over the years, we have adopted a number of dogs from rescues and shelters. First there was Bear and after he passed, Ginger and Scout. Now, we have Kira, another rescue. They have brought immense joy and love into not just into our lives, but into the lives of all who met them.

We want you to know a portion of the profits of this book will be donated in Bear, Ginger and Scout's memory to local animal shelters, parks, conservation organizations, and other individuals and nonprofit organizations in need of assistance.

— Douglas & Sherri Brown,
President & Vice-President of Atlantic Publishing

Table of Contents

CHAPTER 3: Refining Your Idea   61

CHAPTER 4: Rules, Laws, and Playing Well With Others   91

CHAPTER 5: Your First Development   117

CHAPTER 6: The Development Process 179

CHAPTER 10: Related Real Estate Careers

Glossary

Endnotes

Index

1

What Does A Developer Do?

Real estate development is one of the few areas that a person can enter with little expertise and become wealthy in a short time. With the right financial backing, a little business savvy, and careful attention to detail, you too can earn whatever you want to earn.

The Real Estate Development Market

The housing market crash of 2007 was the worst in the U.S. to date. In 1995, the housing market started growing at a steady rate. Then, in 2000, the housing bubble truly began to grow as people began investing more money in real estate as opposed to stocks. As a result, the prices of houses started to climb and people were clambering to both sell at these new prices and buy before the prices got even higher.

Trying to meet this demand for houses, mortgage companies relaxed their standards. In 2007 demand lessened and the value of houses began to drop. Many recent home buyers found themselves owing more than their houses were currently valued at. These homeowners were then either forced to sell their houses at a loss, remain in an underwater mortgage, or default on their mortgage.

Between 2007 and 2012, four million houses were foreclosed on, but the housing market has slowly made its way toward a recovery. From June 2014, to June 2015, there was a 30% increase in housing.

Background

You may be wondering whether you have, or can acquire, the skills of a developer. It is true that good developers must multi-task without letting go of the overall project goal. Developing property with any degree of success relies on interacting well with key players. The steps taken by a typical developer involve working through regulatory channels, the political arena and gaining neighborhood approval. It requires good negotiating skills and luck. Self-knowledge and creativity are both keys to the success of a real estate development project. In addition, there are many steps from the conception of the project to the final stages that involve contracts with a myriad of people, including buyers, sellers, lenders, contractors and architects — so that people skills are high on the list of requirements.

A real estate developer can loosely be defined as a person, partnership, or other entity who has an idea for development and subsequently gathers the seed capital to begin the project, purchases a piece of land or a building, and creates the necessary steps for the project to make a profit. As you delve into your first few projects, you may find that you possess a talent for one part or another. You might begin to specialize in a particular area, or you may search for partners to round out the total process with you.

A developer can also be defined as someone who purchases an existing property and renovates it or revamps it for a different use. Often these properties' use has become obsolete through changes in the market, changes in the neighborhood, or simply due to lack of maintenance and updates. Some areas of the country have a tremendous amount of property revitalization. The fact is that the majority of owners as well as tenants have no idea what a property could look like with renovation or cosmetic upgrades. If you are able to visualize updates to an existing property and you can keep the project cost effective, you may be able to put your ideas into action.

Real estate development projects are unalike because there are so many niches, such as developing raw land or renovating existing buildings. You may have a property in mind where you want to build posh upscale homes, or you may want to create a minimalist office building from the ground up. You may choose to sell your improved parcels to others, or lease and manage them yourself, or put any other combination of all the above ideas into play. With development, you can invent your own job from an array of endless possibilities.

Whether developers are interested in land, multifamily residential, office, industrial, retail development, or mixed-use properties, there are always numerous opportunities. Most developers choose to specialize in a particular segment of these general areas; for example, building strip malls will differ somewhat from building regional malls.

Developers you know may differ widely in their skills, their ego and the level of visibility that they prefer. Developers may choose to concentrate on one type of property or several. They may work in a small niche, regionally or nationally. One who has skills in construction may choose to act as general contractor as well, and another whose background is in finance may choose to hire out that portion of their project. Some choose to work alone, and some choose to work in partnership with others. All developers have a few things in common, though: they must have access to land and capital, and they must have, or develop, skills for management and entrepreneurship.

Education

There are many programs leading to bachelor's degrees, MBAs, and certifications in various aspects of real estate. Columbia Business School, for example, offers an MBA in real estate that combines the hands-on experience of an internship with courses in finance and negotiations. Georgia State University's degrees range from an undergraduate degree in real estate to an MBA, an MSRE, and a PhD in real estate. A listing of a few college programs in real estate development is given at the end of this chapter; it is not complete. New programs are cropping up all the time, so a person who is interested in developing the educational end of their experience could start with local colleges and universities to find classes. Many courses are also offered online, or with "low residency" so that you can do some course work at home and spend minimal time on campus to fulfill your requirements. These schools work hard at fine-tuning their programs to offer a complete education program that will fit the student for the job.

For every person who obtains a degree in real estate, there is one who has no formal training. In fact, until the 1970s, there really were no programs that offered a college-level concentration in real estate. Some professionals say that about 70 percent of what a developer needs to know has to be learned in the field. If you are not trained in the business, do not be intimidated by others who are. Education is only one of many tools that can prepare you for the business.

Real estate development is not for amateurs, yet it can be accomplished successfully by people from all walks of life. According to the Urban Land Institute, the average developer may have a background in accounting, business, real estate, construction, lending, project management, or be a student. Your background alone does not determine the likelihood of your success. Real estate developers create the very basis of urban life as we know it. Their dreams become a reality that changes our landscape for years to come.

Many developers begin by working as an apprentice for someone else to gain knowledge of the field before striking out on their own. If this is your plan, you should be aware from the outset that some employers will want you to have an advanced degree, an MBA or equivalent, and corporate experience. If you are considering working for someone else, experts agree that you can go into any part of the process that fits you and your capabilities, because you can move from one area to another easily. It does not seem to matter whether you start in private or public company; you can learn well in either.

There are more than five million professionals in the real estate field. A great many professional developers have worked their way up the ladder without the benefit of these tools, so do not give up on the dream without exploring all of the options available to you.

Traits of a Developer

A developer is someone who is very active in the process. People who invest but do not participate are investors; people who find tenants or buyers and receive a commission are brokers. Development is different from investment due to the degree of ownership. It is different from being a broker because of the personal risk involved. In developing, you have total control, yet no control at all; you risk everything, and you may gain more than would ever be possible in any of the other connected roles; and perhaps more than in any other career, you rely a great deal on instinct.

Although most of the skills you will need can be learned through reading, taking classes, or by learning on the job, there are a few traits that you must have from the beginning, and I would like to mention those here. If you do not have them, they can be acquired.

- **Being a developer means you have a drive to succeed.** You are excited about your work, and it shows. You get a high from the challenge of the game itself. You thrive on risk, and you push to be the best that you can be on every level.

- **Being a developer requires a great deal of flexibility.** Developers have to shift strategies quickly. They make changes simply to cause the project to meet public approval. They hire and fire employees, renegotiate financing, and contract with buyers or tenants. Deadlines will move forward and back, or simply become unattainable due to circumstances beyond all control.

- **Being a developer means having or acquiring skills in marketing, supervision, finance and risk management.** At any point in the process, a developer may be acting as creator, promoter, negotiator, or investor. They must market to tenants, buyers and the public. They supervise the entire design and construction team. They work with investors and lenders. They cope with the internal pressures associated with high risk on a daily basis.

- **It is almost a given from the previous bullet point:** good developers have self discipline and do not dive into a deal without knowing the details; they are organized and methodical in selecting the next project. They accept disappointment as part of the game and move forward without letting the unforeseen get in the way.

- **Being a developer means having tenacity.** It is a complex business requiring a complex entrepreneur at its helm. Developers have to assemble the talents, manage individuals, make things happen, withstand intense pressure and uncertainty, lead, coordinate, and give their team a clear vision. A developer must be able to sell his idea to his team and to the public. He must have the common sense to know to let go when the risk is too great and outweighs the benefits.

Over and over, real estate developers whom I have talked to in preparation for this book have told me that you must be willing to continue to learn. John Condas, an attorney with Nossaman LLP,

Craig Evans, of CP Development, LLC

Craig Evans started his business as a licensed Realtor selling single family homes. In his first year, Craig says that he met a fairly well-established local home builder and ended up marketing spec homes for him, primarily custom homes. Craig learned from the sales side of the business how the development process worked.

He watched home builders, representing them on custom homes and spec homes. He then found a partner and began a project in Salem that he refers to as "minor partitioning" of land inside a small town. The partitioning consisted of developing three lots at a time.

"After I had some success with that, I moved on up to my first subdivision in an outlying community, assembling several eight- to 10-acre tracts of land in the Dallas, Oregon, area."

Craig says "I have been blessed to have good opportunities and a good market place that has been receptive. Of course, I am still learning and growing."

What does Craig wish he had known in the beginning? "Procedural issues," he says. "I had to learn how politics enters into the process. The temperament of the city was pretty negative, and they were reluctant to allow development when we did that first partition. It was a real challenge to get anything done. Since then, things have evolved, and there is a much more positive environment now as far as development goes."

Does he have any special advice for newcomers to the business?

"As you are going through the approval process, do not take the government employees' word, or the authorities' interpretation of the codes. They interpret as they like instead of getting the codes out and reading them. We were finally able to get help from them by following the codes."

In fact, Craig says, "In our first development we allowed one of the planning department higher ups to convince us that a portion of our land could not be developed. It was not intentional. It was a matter of misinterpreting the code. We did not have the sense to read it or to get an attorney, and it cost us a couple of years because we held the land longer than necessary."

said, "The most important personality trait is to accept that you are not perfect and then be open to learning. Developers should admit that it is a learning process. In fact, the most successful developers that I have worked with are the ones who are content to be generalists, and then rely on experts to do the detail work."

It is a detail business. Be willing to triple check every detail. Otherwise you can easily work for several years on a project and make no money because of a few small mistakes. Ultimately, you are responsible for zoning changes, even if they take place as a result of public pressure; skipped or overlooked tests; undiscovered land issues; and false promises that may arise out of your transaction.

Personal Skills for Success

To analyze your skills, consider the following:

- Do the words "hands on" describe your preferred working style?

- Are you prepared in most of the areas described in the previous section, or are you willing to get the education and experience to handle them?

A developer needs to learn how to work with the other players in the process. Donna Jones of Sheppard Mullin Richter & Hampton in San Diego, CA, said there was one thing she was unaware of at the beginning of her career. "I wish I had known how important it is to build relationships with the various agency decision makers and staff as well as various consultants, and rather than focusing on just the legal issues at the beginning I would have begun developing my network of relationships sooner."

Ms. Jones adds that if there is one thing a first-time developer should try to avoid, it is trying to do everything by yourself.

"Use your contacts and your consultants and their contacts. Do not underestimate how long it will take to obtain your entitlements or complete the development. It generally takes twice as long as you would like at a minimum. Also be diligent with follow up."

Real estate development is an evolutionary process. Beginners have to work twice as hard as seasoned professionals. They will spend more time, risk more and learn more. Most people who go into this kind of work are so enthralled with the business that they are more than willing to undergo the necessary learning curve.

- If not, are you able to hire others who can oversee those areas for you?

- Thinking about your previous or current career, do you find that you complete projects on time with little to no supervision?

There are certain things that will be required. For example, a developer needs to be able to meet a schedule, complete the job correctly, and remain reasonably close to the proposed budget.

A good real estate developer will realize that the public is his or her partner. Treating the public with respect will prevent a multitude of unnecessary problems. In other fields entrepreneurs merely obtain a local business license or a sales tax number, and their career is on the way. The developer has to present the product over and over, exposing it to an overwhelming array of local regulations and political and community approval processes. Consulting with local government, becoming involved with the public, and listening to their concerns are all part of a good working relationship with the community. A developer must understand urban dynamics, even if he or she is just starting out.

A developer must possess negotiation skills. Not all negotiations are about capital; they can involve an agreement with one of your contractors on how to proceed or simply approval from one of your partners. The results of many transactions may seem concrete, but most of the time they are not; there are many possible outcomes from any given negotiation. Learning to recognize all the possibilities and the value of those outcomes to the parties involved is crucial to your relationships with the community, investors, banks, partners and employees.

A developer must provide for long-term operations management. Designing with the end in mind ensures both profitable operations and a long-term expectation of economic value. A comprehensive management plan serves the community better by offering an ongoing positive contribution.

You must have at least a basic knowledge of architecture, construction, law and public finance. You should also have the basic real estate skills of finance, marketing and property management.

A developer must know his own risk level. Every deal has risk, and there may come a point where the risk is too much. Being willing to take calculated risks is part of the job, but the amount of risk is individual to the project. A developer needs to know what percent of risk to bear based on the current financial situation.

The Art of Persuasion

Effective persuasion is the result of knowing how to negotiate. Decisions must be reached, and you evaluate and reevaluate based on your position on the subject, your relationship to the other party, and the level of importance you place on the situation at hand.

Learning to negotiate in a business setting takes skill. You should also learn about the other businesses that you will be negotiating with. You are going to work with lenders, for example, so learn about the lending process and how bankers view developers' loan packages. You will also spend time working with sellers so you'll need to learn assess their position. Learning to negotiate improves every area of the business—from purchase to negotiating for financing to negotiating for the best sale price.

To prepare for a negotiation and persuade the other side to your point of view consider these steps:

PREPARATION

Think about the outcome you desire, other possibilities, and how change affects the outcome you want. Some people write down their good/better/best outcomes with possible variations on each one.

In planning your presentation, take it apart and study each step. Decide on your strategy to get the person to reach the conclusion you want. Plan on receiving objections, and remember, objections are a sign of interest. They may offer objections one on top of the other, in rapid succession, and then suddenly agree to your terms. Therefore, you need to consider what their objections may be and how you will respond to them.

UNDERSTAND YOUR OWN NEEDS

Establish your limits in advance. What will you accept? What is totally unacceptable? Usually, the negotiated contract falls somewhere between your rejection phase and your best case scenario.

Find the value to you of all possible outcomes. As you negotiate, you should keep updating yourself on your Best Alternative to a Negotiated Agreement (BATNA) and your Zone of Potential Agreement (ZOPA). As the contract is negotiated, different components will rise and fall in terms of importance. Keeping your own terms in front of you, at least mentally, helps you to keep the goal clearly in mind and negotiate for what is really important.

KNOW YOUR SUBJECT MATTER

Be willing to go into detail to show that you know all sides of the story. Investigation into recently sold properties, seller attitudes, regional trends, tenant needs, or investor positions pays off! Showing that you have already covered the bases will help the other side to relax. It also builds trust.

RECOGNIZE WHERE YOU ARE

Acknowledge that negotiations you enter into as a developer are different from most other forms of negotiation. If you were purchasing a single piece of real estate, a private residence for example, you would negotiate with the seller for one transaction only—and you would be finished. When it is your business at stake, though, every move you make affects your reputation. So you want to negotiate in good faith. Maintaining professionalism at all times is a must for good business relations.

LEAVE YOUR EGO IN THE CAR

Successful negotiators know that their ease and comfort level actually work against them. Sellers, especially private owners, become suspicious of your experience and abilities. Making fast decisions, refusing to ask for concessions that you clearly need, and never asking approval from a partner or other party are NOT ways to endear yourself to the other side. Instead, carefully treat the other party as if they were your partner or a good friend. If you are trying to establish communication and build trust, the sincerity of your efforts is usually apparent to the other parties even if they do not acknowledge them.

LISTEN CAREFULLY

Skilled negotiators say that when you think you know the other side's view, you usually only know about one-third of it. Make it a point to know their position and the reasons behind it. Visualize the issue from their viewpoint to help you lead them toward your conclusion. Some experts say that pretending the person is a relative or close friend can help you to understand their stance.

ALLOW PLENTY OF SILENCE BEFORE YOU SPEAK

Trust is delicate, hard to win and easily lost. The silence that you allow may help you to re-frame your statement and build (rather than lose) trust.

BE CREATIVE

Because you have done your homework, you know how to repackage attractively for the other party. Be ready to show your flexibility and make trade-offs. You can give a higher price in exchange for performance clauses or a lower down payment.

KEEP CONTROL OF THE CONVERSATION

Think about how to communicate your points if the other party's attention wanders or the conversation drifts. Bringing them back around to the point at hand is something to be done gently. If the entire room breaks off into small talk, it is okay to be silent for a few minutes as you think about your BATNA.

Use a respected authority like the lender or another third party to help neutralize the conversation. Rather than asking, "Would you be willing…" asking "Do you think your investors would be willing…" Taking that one step back from the personal issue allows the other side to remain calm; he does not have to say no himself.

Stay focused. Respect the relationship and the other person. Even as emotions run high, try to separate the person from their position or their actions. People do strange things when they are under pressure and remaining calm places you in a position of more power.

Be familiar. Find the common ground between yourself and the others in the room. Small talk is nearly as important as your persuasiveness; it helps you to establish a relationship. Just as important as the common ground is the commonality—speech patterns and mannerisms. If you are dealing with a sharp, fast-talking executive, match her style and way of speaking. You will find that this makes you seem more "on the same wavelength" so that she will listen to you more closely.

Do not push. Never forget that the relationships you forge now are a part of an ongoing journey. Do your job well, and there will be further opportunities to hone your skills.

Leave the door open. Situations change. People change. Goals change. Allowing room for a graceful re-entry by the other party may work in your favor. For example, you are the first developer to approach a couple who is thinking of selling their farm. Although you offer them $300,000, far more than the farm is worth, they think, "Wow. If he has arrived 15 minutes after the sign is up, imagine how many people will be here this week! We are going to make tons of money! In fact, since he is a developer, that means he is probably offering us LESS than the property is worth. We will just say no and wait for the next buyer."

Imagine this scenario: You graciously thank them for their time. You take the time to indulge in small talk, and share your business card. "I know a thing or two about developing property like this," you tell them. "If you have any questions, feel free to call me."

Months later, when the couple has received no other offers (or lowball offers) your offer seems much more attractive. Because you were careful to leave the door open, they feel comfortable in calling you to see if you are still interested in making an offer.

Kindness is the real winner. Be courteous, even after the deal is signed, and congratulate the other side on their negotiation. Maybe you did not get everything you wanted, and maybe they did not either, but you can honor them with the perception that they "won."

No matter how carefully you hone your negotiating skills, there will be someone, sometime sitting on the other side of the table who simply will not play the game. It is difficult to play ball when the other team is sitting on the ground! Here are some examples.

"Just under the deadline." This negotiator hands you a draft of the contract one hour before the deadline. He or she believes that, because your deadline is looming, you will be more likely to meet his demands. You can offset this by creating a deadline for contract review that is before your final deadline.

"Good cop/bad cop." This is a team of negotiators, one of whom takes the hard core stand, while the other pretends to "make up" for his or her misbehavior. If this happens to you, consider calling them on it.

"The loyal employee." This person states that the offer should be acceptable to you because it is "standard." He or she might as well finish that with, "you moron." In fact, nothing in real estate development is standard. The deal you are negotiating can be whatever the two parties agree to make it.

"I am not in charge." The person claims they do not have the authority to make decisions or alter the terms of the contract. If this happens to you, simply stop and wait until someone who does have the authority can meet with you.

"I am the big dog." This person expects to make all the terms, and expects you to sign the contract with no negotiation. He or she does not understand the concept of win-win. In extreme situations, it might be best to walk away from this non-negotiator. There will be other lenders, sellers, investors and deals.

NEGOTIATING TOOLS THAT YOU CAN USE IN YOUR FAVOR:

Choices

It is always possible that you are not the first person to recognize a great deal, and the seller has 10 other qualified developers making a better offer than you are, but let us suppose that is not the case. Mentioning (at the right moment) that you are looking at other properties or have a better buy in mind will give him or her the perception that you may have more options than he does.

Willingness to Walk Away

If you are negotiating and you are not willing to walk away, you might as well stop negotiating and just hand over the terms the other party is asking for. Locking yourself in mentally before the negotiations puts you on the losing end. You need to be willing to walk away — graciously of course — if you want to get anywhere.

OPPORTUNITIES FOR DEVELOPMENT:

- Single family homes
- Multi-family units
- Assisted living facilities
- Office buildings (suburban)
- Office buildings (central business district; high-rise)
- Strip malls
- Regional malls
- Self storage facilities
- Warehouse distribution buildings
- Manufacturing facilities
- Research and development facilities
- Flex facilities with the previous three building types
- Showroom buildings

Note that within each of these sectors is a further opportunity for specialization.

2

Pre-development

How do you successfully apply negotiating skills to your very first real estate venture and create profitable sales from the start?

Pre-development is the entire period from your first glimpse of the development site to the beginning of construction. Ideally, this period would be only four or six months, which lowers both your cost and the risk involved. However, it is difficult to begin construction while the land deal is closing, especially for a developer who is working on a first project. In the meantime, you must be sure you can carry the debt load that is required to make your dream a reality.

Preparation

You should obtain a license to do business under your business's name. You should also obtain insurance that offers adequate coverage for the task and find an attorney to help sort out all the many details that are involved.

"An attorney finds the things that you might overlook," John Condas, Esq., explained. "Look at it this way: you will get a bigger bill if you wait until you have a mess before you talk with us. It is best to let us handle the things we know how to handle up front."

Craig Evans agrees that good legal advice is necessary to set up a real estate development company properly. "It is an ongoing process," he says. "Make sure you are licensed, insured and incorporated. Get legal advice on everything. It is easy to try to shortcut those things, but you will pay in the end."

The key to a successful real estate development is preparation at every stage. As you become more experienced you will recognize questions and issues before they arise. For now, make the best preparation you can for every meeting and phone call that you make. For example, before you attend a meeting with clients, anticipate their questions and be ready with solutions. Before a meeting with the public, prepare answers and blueprints that spell out a response to their concerns. Before meetings with lenders, gather all the documentation and data you think they will need. Anticipate the concerns of all parties involved as much as you can, and be ready to speak to their needs.

Talking with other developers and studying their history will give you a fairly good idea of the questions that arise from all fronts, and the way that you can respond to them. Most developers agree that the best way to learn is to jump in and begin. There is no formula for success, and there are no two projects that are alike, so expect to always be learning on the job.

In any development process, there are different levels of risk to consider. For example, a low-risk undertaking might involve your being an agent, managing a project for owners or investors. High risk might be investing all the money that goes in and out of the development and taking on all the personal liability. Most first developments fall somewhere in between.

Your first development will be the hardest one of your life. You will encounter more challenges, spend more time, and work harder than in any other development you set out to create, but know that once this one is behind you, there will never be another development as difficult, bewildering, and time consuming. You will never again be a newcomer to the field. You will never have to create all the relationships necessary for the business or work so hard at getting clients, funds and approvals.

It is important to create exactly the type of business atmosphere you plan to have from the outset because the first development sets the tone for how you will do business in the future. You are establishing an image with people you will encounter again: contractors, bankers and investors. So with that in mind, it is important to:

- Do your research well and do not be tempted to latch on to the first development opportunity that you see.

- Create a positive image.

- Be as informed as possible before approaching the professionals you will partner with.

- Always behave in a courteous, friendly manner.

According to Craig Evans, "It is important not to be combative, but ask questions of the resource people, for example inside the public works and city planning staff. Just build relationships and ask for assistance. If you stay positive you can get further. With that said, if you can read codes yourself, interpret them and then act. Do not let them push you around. They will use their power to accomplish their agenda."

Create a Business Plan

Every startup business has to create a business plan. The business plan consists of a narrative, several financial worksheets and a summary. The narrative is the most important part.

Creating a really tight business plan takes several weeks, but having a thorough document for your business is important to your future success.

The best way to create your business plan is to write out each section in paragraphs and edit it. A business plan is a valuable tool because it forces you to research and think about your business in a systematic way. As you plan, you will think back over your ideas in a critical way—plus your research may turn up something that you did not know. So a well-crafted business plan can actually save you time in the long run.

Elements of a Winning Business Plan

COVER SHEET

This is page one and it includes:
- Your Business Name
- Address
- City, State, ZIP Code

- Telephone
- Fax
- Email

TABLE OF CONTENTS

EXECUTIVE SUMMARY

Write this section last. An executive summary can be a few paragraphs to a couple of pages in length, but it should never be more than two pages. This is the part of your business plan that potential investors will circulate among themselves, so it should be clear and concise.

The executive summary should fully explain your business, but keep in mind that people want to grasp it quickly. You want to catch their attention.

Explain all the fundamentals of your business. Describe your target market, your partners if there are any, and what you project for the future of your company. Be enthusiastic, but be very professional.

ADDITIONAL TIP

When you use this document to apply for a loan, add information about how much you want, precisely how you are going to use it, and how the money will enhance your operation.

DESCRIPTION OF YOUR COMPANY

Mission Statement: Many companies have a brief mission statement (two or three sentences) explaining why they created the company and their plans for it.

Company Goals and Objectives: Goals are broader terms about where you want your business to go. Objectives are the smaller steps to get to that goal.

Business Philosophy: What is important to you in business?
Who is your target market?
How will you reach them?

Describe the real estate development industry as you see it. Is it a growth industry? What changes do you foresee in the industry, short term and long term? How will you meet the trends of the industry?

Describe your most important strengths and skills. Why do you believe your company will succeed? How will you deal with competition? What are the key strengths of your firm? Which type of ownership will you have? How did you select this business model?

PRODUCTS AND SERVICES

Describe in depth your products or services (technical specifications, drawings, photos, sales brochures, and other lengthy items belong in Appendices). List all the features as well as the benefits of each of those features.

What factors will give you competitive advantages or disadvantages? Examples include level of quality or unique or proprietary features. What are the pricing, fee, or leasing structures of your products or services? Also list any after-market services, like warranties and maintenance that you offer.

MARKETING PLAN

Any business that is going to sell a product has to have a marketing plan. If you are constructing office buildings that you will lease before you sell, explain how that process will work, and when/how you will market them.

Begin by talking with real estate agents, brokers, lenders and other people in the business to see how they advise that you create your marketing scheme. Do not discount fellow developers! They are the people who can tell you the most about what works for your area and your proposed project.

To create your plan, you should perform research in the industry by reading trade publications, magazines, newspapers, and studying the demographics for your area. This kind of research can be done through your local chamber of commerce, the local builder's organization, as well as the library.

A strong marketing plan contains very specific information; it contains statistics and cites sources. In your marketing section include:

- The size of your market and what percentage of it you think you will have. Describe your target market in detail; give the characteristics of the group and pinpoint their geographic location.

- Demand for your product, with plenty of documentation. Of course, if you are building industrial warehouses, for example, you will have less information about your clients, but you can describe local businesses as a potential customer group to create a demographic profile.

- Information about your company's potential for growth, given the current market conditions and consumer trends.

- Challenges your company may face, like capital, financing issues, and marketing costs. Do not be afraid to address the negatives! This lets your reader know that you have done your research and that you have a good grasp of what you will be up against. Describe how you will address these challenges. Mention any special skills that you have that will help you overcome them. Explain what you will do if the economy changes and how that will affect your project.

Be sure to describe the image that you want to project, and how you believe your customers will view your type of development.

COMPETITION

Who is your competition? List potential competitors in detail, including their names and business addresses. Tell how they will compete with you and how your product will compare with theirs. List your competitive advantages and disadvantages.

Next, describe your strategy for developing your own unique product. How will you promote it? How will customers find you? List all radio, television, print, and Internet media that you intend to use. Explain why you will use each one, and how often. Describe the lowest cost ways to use your budget. Are there other ways to promote your business, like word of mouth, open houses and networking? How do you plan to use them?

Describe all the products that will support your brand, like logos, business cards, letterhead, brochures, signage, and interior design. Get price estimates so that you can offer a realistic budget for them.

List your promotional budget and how many of the items above are a part of it. Break it down by no-cost versus cost, and also by pre-construction, during construction, and post construction budget.

PRICING

Considerable thought must go into the prices you set for your products. Conduct a market analysis and use the documentation from both sold and on-the-market properties to support your pricing methods.

Compare the prices you have gathered with competitors' prices, and explain where your prices fit in the analysis and why. Talk about how important price is (or is not) to your customers.

One of the biggest parts of this section is the creation of a sales forecasting spreadsheet. Using all the information you have just given about your product, the market, and your customers, create a month-by-month projection for your first year. Use the numbers from your marketing plan and planned or historical sales. The forecast should include both a best and a worst case scenario, with an estimate for both.

ADDITIONAL TIP

Keep copies of all the research data you used to support this spreadsheet, and anything that shows assumptions or calculations you have made. Lenders will want to see them.

OPERATIONAL PLAN

This section explains the daily operation of the business. List its location, processes, partners, employees and any equipment you own. Describe your construction methods, quality control, inventory control and any customer service procedures.

Estimate all your operations costs. These may include rent, maintenance, utilities, remodeling costs, and insurance. Describe your office hours and who will be in your office while you are at the job site.

List all your permits and licensing, including:

- Licensing and bonding requirements

- Special regulations or permits required in your area

- Zoning requirements

- Health and workplace regulations

- Insurance coverage

Include a section about personnel, including number of employees, types of laborer (skilled or unskilled), and how you intend to obtain employees. Explain who will be independent contractors and who will be employees. Talk about the existing staff, if there is any, and your pay structure. If you have already created your employee handbook, include that here.

Next, create an inventory section. List all the tools and equipment you have, the value of your inventory, and where you intend to store it. Identify all building supplies as a separate section of the inventory, and identify your key suppliers by name and address. List their credit policy and mention whether they deliver products to you. Describe your history with each company. Mention what you will do in response to dramatic fluctuations in the prices of supplies.

MANAGEMENT AND ORGANIZATION

If the business is not a sole proprietorship, who will manage the daily operations? List his or her expertise and include a résumé. Describe the employee structure in your organization. If your company is large enough, include an organizational chart. When you use the business plan to apply for loans, attach the résumé for yourself, your partners and all management.

Also list in this section everyone who functions as support for your business, even though they are not on your regular payroll. The list may include your attorney, accountant, insurance agent, banker or other lenders, consultant, and any other key advisors.

PERSONAL FINANCIAL STATEMENT

Include personal financial statements for yourself, each owner and major stockholders. Show all your assets and liabilities held outside the business as well as your personal net worth.

STARTUP EXPENSES AND CAPITALIZATION

Describe where you plan to get your startup expenses, including the funds for your first venture. Refer back to the section on seed capital if you need to. Be very clear and open about the way you plan to finance your first project, even if the plan involves something as simple as using all your credit cards.

In addition to the cost of the project, you will have many new business start-up expenses. List all of these and add a little bit of padding to each because there are always more expenses than you expect. Create an extra line item, miscellaneous or contingencies, to allow for overages. This line item probably should equal 15 percent to 20 percent of all the other expenses. If you are not sure how much to allow for all this, try to find a developer who is fairly new and still remembers his original start-up costs.

At the end of your expense statement, explain what research you used to arrive at these numbers. List the source of any loans you have already gained approval for, the amounts and the terms. Describe your investors, including the size of each investor's contribution.

FINANCIAL PLAN

A financial plan is simply a 12-month profit and loss projection. You should include a cash-flow projection, a balance sheet, and a break-even summary. Optionally, it may include a five-year profit and loss projection to give the reader an overall view of your company's financial state.

The 12-month profit and loss statement is simply where you take all your sales projections, cost of goods sold, expenses, and profit and put them together. It is considered the main part of the plan for many businesses, but in a business like yours where you may not see a return for several years down the road, it may not be as important.

Include a narrative explaining all the assumptions for the given model and describe what will be happening during months that you are not making a profit. If you are just starting the business, do not be afraid to state that you are operating at a loss!

A five-year projection, should you choose to include one, will simply take forecasts of market data and combine them with your key assumptions about your own projects. Of course, you cannot know everything that is going to happen with the market or the economy, but if there are any large planned changes, this is an opportunity to list them.

CASH FLOW

Create a cash flow projection to sum up how much your start-up costs are, including pre-construction expenses, operating expenses and reserves. This is one part of your business plan that you will want to keep referring back to and keep updating. By continually studying your cash flow, you will be alerted to any changes or shortfalls in time to head them off, either by cutting back on costs or by rearranging your financing.

PROJECTED CASH FLOW

If the profit projection is the heart of your business plan, cash flow is the blood. Every part of your business plan is important, but none of it means a thing if you run out of cash.

The point of this worksheet is to plan how much you need before startup, for preliminary expenses, operating expenses, and reserves. You should keep updating it and using it afterward. It will enable you to foresee shortages in time to do something about them, perhaps cut expenses, or perhaps negotiate a loan. But foremost, you should not be taken by surprise.

List all regular expenses, like quarterly tax payments, as well as maintenance, repairs, inventory payments, loan payments, equipment purchases and withdrawals you plan to take from the business.

From your startup expenses, you should be able to create a balance sheet. A balance sheet lists assets, which are all the items your company owns, and liabilities, which are all of your debts. Your equity is the total of your assets minus your liabilities. For the purposes of getting credit or acquiring investors, you may want to create a projected balance sheet showing how your business should fare at the end of the year.

APPENDICES

This section contains all the supporting documents for the previous sections. Any research, blueprints, plans, demographic studies, forecasting, maps, aerial maps, photographs, articles, and brochures are included here. Attach a list of all equipment you own or that you will purchase, letters of commitment from bankers, leases and contracts, and other supporting materials. If you will use assets as collateral for loans, list those in this section as well.

Congratulations! If you have taken the time to use this as a guide, you have created an entire business plan. This will be a reference document so it is best to store it permanently. Slipping the pages inside plastic sleeves will make them easier to rewrite and replace as the plan is modified. Now on to forming your ideas for development.

Initial Ideas

This is the stage where you let the ideas flow, write them out, and sort them according to whether they can work. As a good entrepreneur, you will find the opportunities that make money — hopefully ahead of the crowd.

Where do you get your ideas? You can get them from a broker or from other developers. You may talk to lenders or other people who are in the field, but you do not have to depend on others to show you where there is potential. Drive around your area; what direction is the city growing in? Is there an area that could be easily revitalized, or in which rehabilitation has already begun? Is there an empty lot surrounded by rising commercial projects or one small farm being dwarfed by high-rise condos?

Learning to anticipate the direction of growth will eventually make you wealthy. At the idea stage, nothing is ridiculous; your market study will determine whether it is viable, anyway. Let your mind wander freely as you make a regular habit of assessing the area with business in mind.

Most cities do not tend to expand in an even pattern around their perimeter; instead, growth occurs along a corridor in a particular direction. The person who can anticipate this direction and begin to develop property right in this pathway is the person who will realize the greatest potential from his or her development. Even if you have to hold onto a property for several years, if you are in the path of growth you cannot help but succeed.

Of course, if you choose to use a broker to help you find ideas, a dedicated broker can be a wealth of information for you. A real estate broker knows what is for sale, what could be for sale soon, and what simply cannot be bought. He has a clear idea of whether a property is a good deal, and he is more than willing to share that information with you. If a broker feels you are a good buyer, one who will purchase the property and get to closing, he will work hard to find properties that meet your needs. Do not be afraid to let your broker know that you are new to the business and you want to start small. The more information you can give him, the more likely he is to find exactly the property that you want.

Even when the broker prepares an attractive sales package, you should make it a habit to double check all the information he gives you. This is where a very hands-on approach pays off for a developer. What assumptions were made to put the package together? Are they valid? Are the figures correct? If he is showing you information about a tenant in a building, for example, go talk to the tenant. Visit with owners, city officials, and online sites that have provided the information he holds. Be sure that what the broker believes to be true actually is true. This habit will take you far; after all, there is already enough uncertainty in this business.

Buying at Auction

People who are new to the business of real estate wonder whether it is okay to buy land or properties at auction. The answer is a qualified "yes." Buying at auction is a great way to get a good deal — if you do your homework.

"There are many types of real estate sold at auction, including residential, land, commercial, and industrial. It is important to know whether you can add value to it, so you have to be prepared ahead of time," said Rob Friedman, of National Recreation Properties, Inc., in San Diego, California.

If you are used to attending antique auctions, you will find that real estate auctions are different in a few respects. Generally, to buy property at an auction you have to register with the auction house ahead of time, and on the day of the auction you should bring them a pre-determined sum of money (you can find this in the sales advertisements for the auction, as well as in the conditions of sale) in the form of a cashier's check or a certified check. Personal checks are almost never accepted. If you are not the winning bidder, the auction company returns your check to you; if you do win, the check becomes your deposit money.

Before the auction, you should inspect it. Normally you do this by making an appointment with the agent. Familiarize yourself with all the terms and conditions of the sale, and any other paperwork that is available. If you are going to have someone else bid for you, the person will need to supply the auctioneer or agent with a written document stating that they have the authority to do the bidding.

It is important to obtain approval for financing ahead of time, if necessary. Unlike many other kinds of purchases, auctions usually are not contingent on the buyer's ability to acquire financing. If you are unable to go through with the sale you will lose your deposit. Usually the terms of an auction are 10 percent down with settlement to be held within 30 days. By bidding, you are agreeing that you have the ability to pay for the property and complete the contract.

The final decision of whether you win the auction, even if you are the highest bidder, is based on two things: the reserve price and the seller's approval. Normally all properties are subject to a reserve price. If you have not met the reserve, then the auction is not completed. It is important to remember that there is no cooling off period with real estate auctions; you do not get to change your mind later!

The purchase of property at auction is usually not contingent on any sort of inspection process, either. Most auctions use the language "as is, where is," which means you are buying the property as it stands, regardless of any sort of tests that the property may fail.

The auctioneer has the right to refuse a bid from any person; the decision is final, so you will not have a way to dispute it. In the event that there is a dispute on a bid, the auctioneer will probably simply re-open the bidding at the highest amount that was accepted.

One of the most important pieces of information to learn before the day of auction is the real value of the property. You generally cannot judge the value by the starting price of the auction; many people believe the auctioneer's opening price reflects the worth, but remember that the auctioneer's job is to get as much as possible for the property. Getting a valuation is well worth the time and inconvenience if you are making a large investment.

Real properties that are up for sale do not have to be held until auction day; often the sellers will consider offers that are presented before the auction. When you register with the auction house to show your interest in the property, they will be able to contact you to meet any bids from others.

To bid at auction successfully,

- Visit a few auctions first to learn how they work

- Familiarize yourself with the property before the auction

- On auction day, arrive a little early

- Do not bid at the opening of the bidding process

- Attract the auctioneer's eye by raising your hand or catching his eye

- Remember your budget and do not exceed it

What About Online Auctions?

These are even more iffy than attending an auction in person. Purchasing property online is quite a risk because there may be structural or environmental issues that cannot be corrected. The property also could be inaccessible for various reasons—either for physical reasons or because it is land locked with no right of way granted.

Nevertheless, more properties are going up for sale at auction. Some sellers take online bids and accept a deposit and then offer you financing; others simply sell the property outright. eBay and other auction companies like it are actually not licensed to sell real estate, so your bid there is not legally binding. Rather, you can indicate your intent to purchase and then hold a meeting with the seller after the auction to hammer out a contract to purchase.

Market Research

Market research is the starting point for any development. Before you can create a desirable product, you must fully understand your market and all its players—those who use the property, those who purchase property and the tenants. Building a project without first knowing the market can serve your own dreams and desires, but in the end it may not be very profitable!

The word "market" usually means groups of customers. They can be grouped and regrouped in many different ways: geographically, demographically, or by product type. It is useful to group them in these ways to study their needs and demands. For our purposes, the market consists of all your potential customers. They share a particular need (or a want), and they might engage in purchasing your goods or services **if they perceive that those products supply their need.**

Understanding the market means that you are aware of what your customers want and need. By understanding what they want, you can easily position yourself to offer that which will satisfy their demands. Therefore, as you may have guessed, your market study is an ongoing process. You will study your market as long as you remain in the business to establish what people want, and later to be aware of changes in those wants.

One example of the changing market is the way that the U. S. household population has changed. Married couples with children under 18 comprised 40 percent of households in 1970; by 2012, only about 20 percent of households were made up of married families with children under 18. At the same time, the number of single-parent households rose from 11 percent in 1970 to 18 percent in 2012. These changes are significant if you are building residential dwellings, because the type of home that is required will be different.

By the way, as a developer you cannot assume that because

something is new and innovative, it will be successful. What is innovative may not be practical; or it may not have appeal to the particular market you are striving to reach. If it does not succeed, cut your losses early and stop supplying it.

A market study discovers whether the specific proposed project will enjoy future success. It involves developing an understanding of the local and national level of the market and its influencing factors. Trends can be used as forecasts of supply and demand. By understanding both levels of the market clearly, a developer or his marketing team researches and selects target markets using information on customers who have purchased or leased a product that is similar to yours.

When you are familiar with the national data, it is time to turn to the local market study. Let us begin with a study of the present trends. Examining local real estate ads, talking with brokers, and asking other developers will help you find out the types of space that are currently available. Look at their use and intended use, size, location, function, and style. What is similar to your idea? What is different? How do you think the differences affect the plan?

Next, look at the demand. Demand changes with trends and demographics. What are current preferences telling you about your development? Find the five most popular new developments in the area and study them in detail. What is the typical unit size? What are its features and benefits?

When you are comparing rents, do not forget about the vacant lots that are on the market. The possibility of competition is just as important as the current availability, maybe more so, since newer buildings may contain attractive design or other features that renters find appealing.

This is also the time to learn about rents and value. What are the income levels of the typical tenants? Who are the tenants? Office occupancy rates are typically lower than the rates for apartments; generally, a rate of about 90 percent for offices and 95 percent for apartments is considered acceptable.[i] What are the vacancy rates? Working on a project that involves leases as an end result automatically means that vacancy rates are difficult to assess. There are several reasons for this, but most likely there will be leases the developer may not be aware of, rentals that are not full to capacity, and the possibility of subleasing. So it is best to focus on what percentage of a space is being used by tenants, rather than trying to calculate the vacancy rate.

How much turnover should you expect in a given time? What are the operating expenses?

To provide any sort of building that fills a need, zero in on one type of development — for example, a high-rise apartment building — and learn everything you can about that project within your targeted area. Most of the above questions will be answered as the study progresses.

On the societal level, you will want to compare your market opportunity with all the forces that influence society and institutions, meaning you will study technology, demographics, cultural developments, political attitudes, legal changes, and economic trends. All of these studies should be ongoing if you are serious about a career in real estate development. By staying abreast of the trends, you already have a large part of your research out of the way. Reading Internet reports, ezines, newspapers and industry publications will keep you up-to-date.

Another good way to gather information without a great investment of time is to locate industry forecasters and use their data. Forecasters pinpoint emerging trends and point them out, allowing you to use their projections to predict the robust side of the market and the trends in your area.

On the industry level, a market study includes current and potential suppliers, potential customers and your competitors. It will also include a study of the politicians and the public, because these are the people who will regulate your market. Developers look for socioeconomic and behavioral distinctions that separate people into groups. This segmentation forms a distinct combination of people, lifestyles, purchasing power and pace. For example, if you find that everyone who lives in a new development southwest of town is between the ages of 32 and 38, that is a pretty narrow segment. Obviously there is something attractive in the subdivision for that age group. What is it? Can you fill the same need for that age range? What is another target group that has a similar need? By studying these types of patterns, you will know the market.

Determine the ease with which a new project can be initiated in terms of local zoning and politics. The zoning and approvals process can take years, unfortunately.

Also note the size and any physical constraints such as drainage, soil conditions, and land formations like mountains or boulders, and bodies of water.

Finally, you will measure your idea, not solely against the market, but for its viability.

Demographics

By comparing the actions of groups of people to historical patterns, we can see how trends are developing. The distribution of households with certain age, income, mobility, educational levels, and employment status is of particular use to developers, who use the research to predict change.

Where do you find demographic information? You may have a local economic development office, city or regional planning centers, and state government offices. The Bureau of Labor Statistics and the Economic Research Service of the U.S. Department of Agriculture, and the National Planning Association publish estimates of demographics. If you cannot find demographic information, sometimes you can hire a consultant to perform a study for you, particularly if you are interested in a relatively small population, like a particular area of town.

Some demographic trends are easy to predict; for example, the high number of births in the United States between the 1940s and the 1960s spurred a demand for baby clothes and diapers, then a demand for education, and by the 1990s there was a dramatic rise in the number of retired persons.

As a developer, you will be interested in studying the age and labor force of your area to follow trends and understand how lifestyles are changing. For example, baby boomers have created a more active lifestyle for retirement than earlier generations; they have more disposable income, fewer children, and are more apt to own second homes. This is information that definitely affects the size and type of home you would construct if you were a residential developer.

Economic forces and wage rates create a pattern that changes over time; studying the trends gives you a forecast of demand for the market, and ultimately for your particular development.

Regional Shifts

The residential future of cities and outlying areas determines the prevailing type of housing and business districts. Are secondary cities still growing? Does the main city show an increase in residents? How many residents are renters? Where do they tend to cluster?

These demographic shifts, urban sprawl, and a trend toward an environmental ethic have led to a trend called smart growth, which is an attempt to unify an area and avoid the segmentation of urban sprawl. It is the effort undertaken to restore communities and offer them numerous housing options; it combines good environmental use with mixed properties, residential, commercial, and retail. It helps to center the area around the town, giving the residents a renewed sense of place.

Smart growth preserves natural areas inside the cities as well as around the locality to allow for "breathing room," along with wildlife, biological habitats, recreation, working farms, and environmental beauty. Open space preservation boosts the economy, supports the environment, and helps structure the new growth of existing communities.

This chart from the Social Security Administration shows the changes in the workforce as well as predicted changes.

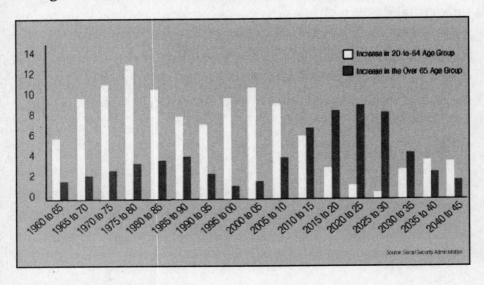

KEEP IT SIMPLE

As a beginning developer, you will probably want to choose a market that is close to home so that you know the area and are familiar with local politics. The knowledge that you already have in the business will assist you in your success. A track record of successful small projects will take you far in the early stages of your career.

To create a successful first development, look for one that can be done in a relatively short period. Look for a "simple" deal — one that is easily within your financial capabilities, even if that means bringing in a business partner. This will help you to make the development a success, which is vital at the front end of your career.

The governing body of the municipality often seems intimidating to the newcomer. Even if you are not a locally based business person (or you have not been up until now), with time and effort you can work your way through the political aspect of development. If you do not know how to "play the game" — you will learn. Land use is determined by local government, so you have no choice in the matter.

Viability

A developer

- has to be reasonably sure that the project will be a success according to his objectives before he signs a purchase contract.

- has to determine whether he can gain all the public approvals necessary to build the project.

- has to obtain appropriate financing.

All of these elements must be in place before you can move forward with your project.

Your main concerns at this stage are the use, location and size of the proposed development. If all of your requirements are met for these three purposes, you can move to a financial feasibility study with reasonable assurance that the project will be a go. No matter whether you are building affordable housing or high-rise office buildings, the facts that affect the site's desirability remain closely the same.

Factors that you will study are:

- Location
- Fit for the proposed use

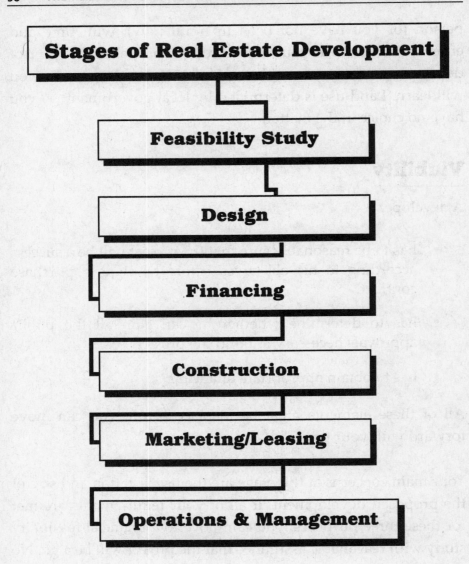

Stages of Real Estate Development

Feasibility Study

Design

Financing

Construction

Marketing/Leasing

Operations & Management

- Accessibility

- Travel time and access to public transportation

- Public improvements

- Neighborhood factors, such as noise, crime, traffic

In determining the feasibility of a development, beginners try to go into too much detail early in the analysis. Remember, market analysis will take place both before and after site selection, so that you will have plenty of time to correct yourself as you move forward.

Developers always have to cope with the fluidity of the project; having too little or too much data, having the market change after the initial market study, or having inaccurate information. Part of your job on the first three or four developments you create will be learning to go with this constant movement, yet remaining focused. Keep up with current trends and be sure to network. This way you will keep your eye on the market and its trends, and you will hear what other people have to say about your project. Return repeatedly to the market study to maintain control of your development process.

By projecting forward you will create a product that responds to future demand rather than the market demand at the time you began. Since the development process can take several years, changes will occur. Where will the economy be in three years? In five? Who is developing the property around your proposed site? What are they building? How will that tie into your plans? Are they a competitor, or will the other development fit awkwardly against yours? These are all questions that help you consider the future market demand. It is prudent to learn all that you can and to keep yourself informed of the changes around you as they occur.

If you are developing land, at this stage you will want to contact firms that build your type of product. They will be a great resource for your feasibility study. You should also contact brokers and lenders who stay current on local market trends and will offer tremendous insight into the feasibility of your project.

3

Refining Your Idea

Your Proposed Site: Best Use

What is the best site for your development? You need to know everything about the various locations in your area and how they correspond to the market you have in mind. You have already learned through the market study what the most desirable areas of town are and the characteristics of the customers who are currently buying there. You will need to know which neighborhoods use public transportation, and which ones enjoy bike trails and walking paths. If you are building an office park, you should study how the employees in the area get to work and how far they drive. For a retail development, you need to know all the shopping habits of the residents.

There are many ways to gather this information, and you should use all of them. You can employ a market consultant, gather information from the local economic development office, and use the Internet to analyze the market. Some developers simply drive to a location that is similar in scope to their proposed site and study the traffic going in and out. Some who specialize in redevelopment spend a day or two at the location examining its strengths and weaknesses for consumers.

You will examine the location and study its desirable traits from the eyes of a potential buyer. For example, how accessible is it from major roads and highways? Is it visible? How close is it to schools, churches and shopping? How easily could the residents reach local parks and other recreational attractions? Put yourself in the shoes of the prospective owner or tenant and imagine the direction the project should take.

Next, a comparison should be done of the surrounding homes or other buildings that are already in existence. Does your proposed project blend easily with the existing environment? If not, how can you make it blend?

Do the surrounding structures have all the utilities? If not, are utilities available? How are they installed and how will that installation fit with your proposed structure? How long will it take?

You also must consider at this time all zoning and regulatory approvals and how the approval process works. Talk with city planners and find out their plans for growth. Ask about existing utilities. You should also learn about all easements.

If you are building single family homes, gather the recent "solds" in your area and break them down by price in each section of town. The breakdown will be in $25,000 or $50,000 increments, depending on your market. Estimate demand by calculating the percentage of all new units sold for the area. For example, let us say that 40 percent of all new housing is being built in the south end of town. Eighty percent of those are priced under $400,000, and the total projected demand in 2016, according to your local economic development council, is 10,000 houses. So you multiply 40 percent x 80 percent x 10,000 = 3,200 new homes needed in the south end of town in your price range.

Preliminary Pro Forma

A pro forma is simply a hypothetical statement that shows income and expenses that can be expected in the future. The pro forma cash flow predicts the flow of cash in and out of your business. Businesses create pro forma statements to make planning decisions, determine the impact of each aspect of the business on the bottom line, and to report to lenders, investors and partners. A pro forma statement can provide these individuals with a basis for understanding the company's financial structure.

The first step of the pro forma process is the financial modeling phase. The pro forma method is a quick, correct, cost-effective method of creating the financial model. The statement will give you data to use for calculating financial ratios to test the goals of your business plan. It will help you to test out the validity of your plan by studying the costs of labor, materials, financing and overhead.

Although the American Institute of CPAs and the Securities and Exchange Commission (SEC) require standard formats for pro forma statements, your preliminary statement will be a draft. Often called the "back of the envelope" pro forma, your very first one will simply be a list of the very basic cash flow pertaining to the project.

Imagine you are considering purchasing an apartment building. Your preliminary pro forma might be as simple as this:

Pro-forma Cash Flow Statement 2017

Projected Rental income: $125,000

Expenses:
  Taxes - $5,800
  Utilities - $25,000
  Miscellaneous - $1,500

Total expenses: $32,300

Cash flow: $92,700

Pro forma statements are an absolute necessity before you invest your time, money and energy. They help you minimize your risks when starting up and running a new business. It is valuable to help you see when you might experience a shortage of cash so that you can decide ahead of time how to improve the cash flow. You might be able to increase your cash through borrowing money, making a draw on a current loan, or cutting expenses. After the initial pro forma, projections must be updated monthly and annually. Base them on reliable, objective information to make the best projection of your profits, losses and upcoming financial needs.

You build the pro forma statement by using certain assumptions about your financial and operating projections. Next, develop the revenue and expense projections. Use those to create the profit and loss projections and then translate the results to the cash-flow projection.

It is vital at this stage to obtain projections from other similar companies and analyze yours against theirs. Each proposed plan or project is unique, and yours will have distinct financial characteristics, but by reviewing others you can make assessments about the impact that marketing, production and other factors have on your profitability.

Feasibility

The financial feasibility study is a procedure for identifying and evaluating the creation, construction and operation of a commercial real estate project. The question you are trying to answer is: Is the project economically viable? A feasibility study really has only two sides: the cost and the income. If you are applying for financing, the investors are going to want to know about both. So the feasibility study is essentially a financial analysis to answer one question: Will your development produce a profit? An understanding of this process helps you to determine whether the project is a go or not.

Many developers spend 10 percent to 20 percent of their time on the feasibility study. It may require up to 15 percent of your total costs—not much, when you compare the value of the study to your overall value of success versus failure.

Common miscalculations by first-time developers include:

- Underestimating costs. You must determine all costs involved and calculate overages into your cost estimates on all levels.

- Underestimating long-term operating expenses.

- Underestimating a reserve to be used for replacement costs.

- Overestimating how much rent you will collect.

- Not making an allowance for tenant turnover.

- Overestimating your ability to raise rent over time.

- Estimating a low cap rate for your sale.

- During lease-up, neglecting to allow an interest reserve.

- Estimating a too-short lease-up time.

Your first feasibility study is going to be the loosest in terms of the financial analysis. The numbers you have at the beginning are the least accurate numbers that you will have through the entire process. When you are thinking about purchasing a piece of property, whether it is land, a building, or some combination of buildings, your cost figures are probably not exact. Right now, before actually making an offer on a piece of property, you have a proposed price and can somewhat project costs. But the land cost — we hope — will turn out to be less than the original asking price, once negotiations are completed. So at this stage, nothing is for sure. Later as the deal becomes firm, you will come back to your financial analysis again to make adjustments. For now, your vision should be based less on finances and size, and more on whether it fits with your company and the community.

There will be several stages of feasibility and at every stage you simply use the best figures you have available at the time. Right now, at the beginning stage where you are just trying to decide whether to buy the land, your figures are general. You would use the full asking price, all associated costs, and calculate from there.

Any price that you negotiate below the original price is safe.

The land costs will include the price, conveyance costs, stamp duties, legal fees, and most likely other fees as well. If your feasibility study shows that you can have a positive profit return for the risk of developing the property, you should proceed with your proposal.

In addition to the cost of the purchase, you want to include figures for the design consultants, architects, and engineers as well as construction costs.

Perhaps you are building homes, and you know you will need to create sales commissions and brochures. So the next item in your feasibility study will be marketing costs. You should also add in the sales commission to real estate agents at this point.

This feasibility study gives you your best estimate of the flow of cash from the lender and from your equity fund. This is called the cost cash flow. In the best case scenario, the cost cash flow is enough to cover the total development costs.

Here is how it works. Let us say that the terms of your development loan tell you the lender will cover 80 percent of your costs. The rest (20 percent) will come from your own equity resources. You can use the 80 percent figure against your monthly expense figure to determine how much interest you will pay to the lender. Now you have the total cost of financing your development. Adding this figure to the total development costs gives you what is called the total capital cost of the development (financing plus development costs).

Now you need to investigate the sales side of feasibility. For the purposes of this section, let's assume that you are creating units to sell; however, many developers maintain their properties as rentals, which creates a very different type of cash flow.

So, sales income is going to be received in exchange for the structure(s) you are building. After deducting the total costs, the total income that is left is your net sales income.

CAUTION: It can be a while before you can get your hands on the sales income!

Let us look at how and why this can happen. Let us say you have hired a builder who built some homes. At the end of the construction project, the builder moves off site. The architect returns to the site and inspects the project. He presents you with a list of defects.

You have to call the builder back to the site to correct the defects, and he in turn calls on the subcontractors, and then the architect returns to complete the final inspection. He will then issue a completion certificate. At this point, further tests have to take place. For example, the surveyor or engineer must take final measurements and compare them to unit plans; the final unit plan may have to be presented for settlement. There are numerous other types of paperwork that may be required, all of which can impact your settlement date.

After the flurry of final items, the lender will arrange to go to settlement. However, the lender gets his payment first. So your equity and your profit will go to you after the debt is paid.

Dollars and Sense

Do you have access to capital? It is fairly easy for a developer with a proven track record to obtain funding from a bank within his area of specialization. But if you are just beginning, you will probably need some funds from another source. You may have your own resources that you can tap into: cash, credit cards, and other forms of personal credit. You may borrow from family members or friends. Even if you obtain lender financing, it is usually just a percentage; it is common for the lender to expect you to front 20 percent or even more of the capital for your project.

Sending out feelers before beginning the project by making phone calls to lenders you already know. If they are interested in lending you money for the project, they will give you a letter of qualification stating the terms of the loan. Banks will usually only issue a construction loan that can be rolled over to a mini-permanent loan. Construction loans, because they are short-term, can be obtained as portfolio loans through the commercial real estate loan department of your local bank.

Nurturing a new business, money-wise, can seem a daunting task. If you do not already have a relationship with a local mortgage banker, you will need to build one. You will need ongoing reliable sources of funds. If the mortgage lender does not have a network of loan officers they can approach, consider using a mortgage broker. Brokers work to bring a borrower to a lender for a successful close; they are paid fees for their roles in such transactions. They can be especially beneficial to a first-time developer, because they can guide you toward an appropriate lender, through the paperwork, and help streamline the process to save time.

If you have a private investor, the person will expect about a 20 percent per year return on their investment; venture capital groups look for an even larger return.

Other methods of borrowing money:

- Pension funds

- Insurance funds

- REITs

- Public debt, like redevelopment loans

- Private grants like nonprofit target grants

- Public grants, such as anti-blight subsidies, affordable housing credits, tax incentives, historic preservation grants

- Equity financing, the use of cash flows from other projects owned by the developer

- Subordination, borrowing against your company's own assets

There is an interesting online lending group called Prosper, **www.prosper.com** that is dedicated to lending money to the average consumer who needs a diversified loan package. They also cater to people who want to lend money. Even as a first-time borrower, you can present your case and lenders will bid on your right to use their funds; you get to choose which deal works for you. Using a group like Prosper helps create capital for your first venture, and builds a relationship (as well as a positive credit portfolio) that you can put to work from now on.

The name of the game at the beginning, at least from the financial side, is to create leverage, which means using someone else's capital to help you get into a deal. Leverage increases your potential profit at the same time that it magnifies your risk. There is usually a period of negative cash flow, and lenders know this.

Why is it difficult to obtain financing for real estate ventures? Real estate is an expensive non-liquid asset. That means the up-front costs are high, ownership costs are high, and there is no guarantee that you can resell it to gain back your investment. Plus, if you are developing it, you will have added costs. Sales are difficult and a return on development is often delayed.

Due Diligence

As you begin your real estate development venture, you are going to hear about due diligence, which is an opportunity for you to study the environmental concerns, expenses, and potential harm your project could have on the surroundings. No matter whether your deal involves extremely complex multiple properties or a small parcel of land, this is a time to investigate and research public records about the property you want.

Every developer who has been through a few transactions has a horror story to share; the majority tell of easements, title problems, or hazardous wastes that show up after the closing. Creating a good process for due diligence may not totally eliminate this sort of problem, but it certainly will help.

Due diligence means uncovering hidden liens, judgments, licensing issues, legal risks, contracts, and any other sort of information that would make the property less desirable. It is a last opportunity to recreate the deal without taking a significant loss on the investment. You must negotiate a due diligence period that is adequate for identifying issues.

Almost all state and federal regulatory agencies keep property databases that include comprehensive data on environmental permits, existing conditions (like contamination) and any remedial actions that may have been taken on the property. Reviewing these databases can help you build your assessment of the property.

You will find that many sellers do not provide all the details that are necessary to answer your questions, especially those about environmental issues. A qualified consultant will quickly find the gaps in their reports and will locate missing information that can give you a more thorough understanding of the scope of the property's risk.

Having a consultant or a team of consultants ready before you begin your project can help you to gather relevant data quickly to make an informed decision. This will mean locating appropriate consultants, tailoring a contract with them that will suit your needs, and creating a confidentiality agreement. It would be a mistake to find the property first, then look for consultants; your due diligence window of opportunity could easily pass by before you agreed on the terms of the consulting contract.

As you follow your due diligence course, several things may happen. One is that a Phase I ESA (Environmental Site Assessment) study may be triggered. This can be a result of uncovering possible contamination, or simply because of the area's industrial history. Depending on the results of the Phase I ESA, a Phase II or Phase III study may be implemented. These studies, although lengthy, will absolve you as the purchaser from future liability due to contamination or other environmental issues; as such you should welcome the assessment.

Due Diligence Checklist

Here is a checklist to help you plan your strategy:

CONTRACT DATA

- Is all the ownership information present on the purchase agreement?

- Is it current and correct?

- Does the purchase agreement contain the real estate agent's name, price, escrow agent, fees and amount of the required deposit?

- Does it indicate which areas are buildable?

- Do you have environmental statements?

- Are all improvements listed?

- Is there seller financing involved? If so, is it written into the agreement?

- If zoning has to be changed to develop the property, did you make the offer contingent upon zoning approvals? *see note

*Note: When you put a contingency on zoning or other approval in a purchase offer and the subsequent contract, be sure that you detail exactly what type of action constitutes approval. If you do not get this approval, the earnest money will be returned to you, so the wording is very important.

TITLE

- Do you have a title report?

- Is it showing clear title?

- Are the taxes on the property (both city and county) current?

- Are there building restrictions, easements, or other agreements in the original deed that would preclude you from accomplishing your purposes?

- Are there crops or crop allotments?

- Do they affect your ability to build?

ENTITLEMENT

- Who is the governing body?

- Are there moratoriums?

- Ordinances

- Zoning

- Is it part of a redevelopment area?

- Are there condemnations?

- Are there any special assessments?

- Do you have a subdivision approval timetable?

ADVERSE CONDITIONS

- How much of the site is buildable? (Check for all of these through new studies and/or prior documentation)

- Topography

- Drainage

- Survey

- Special Zones

- Soil problems

- Flood areas

- Wetlands

- Toxic/hazardous waste

- Vegetation

- Seismic faults

- Adjoining land issues, such as rights of way

- Views

- Access

PRESENCE OF UTILITIES

- Gas

- Electric

- Water

- Wells

- Sewer

- Septic systems

- Telephone

- Cable television access

- Street lights

- Joint trenching

- Storm drainage

- Emergency services

- Trash collection

PROJECT GOALS

- Are you able to build the project you plan to?

- How many units and at what density can you build?

- Can parking and other amenities be built?

- Can you get the financing to complete the project?

- Approval of the general plan

- Approval of design

- Zoning approval

- Variances

- Development agreements

- Building permits

- Tentative tract map

- Final tract

- Site plan approval

Before Application Process

While you are still in the pre-application period, hire the surveyors, engineers, and attorneys who will be part of the team. The process of municipal site plan review and subdivision application will require both development and legal experts, and a surveyor will be necessary to prepare your site plan. Also, if your project involves the potential for environmental impact, such as building on or near wetlands, you will need to employ the services of a wetlands scientist. There may also be consultations with hydrologists, property valuation experts, and/or environmental engineers. Project experts such as these will be able to review the applicable regulatory requirements and draft applications before you file anything with the regulators. Competent experts, accurate and comprehensive studies, and compliant applications will give your local officials and regulators a positive impression of you. Plus, you will avoid costly errors and show them that you are serious about compliance. These steps will help you develop trust in the field as well as improve your chances of getting timely approvals.

The value of an attorney cannot be overemphasized. An experienced, qualified land use attorney will serve as your project coordinator as well as the regulatory liaison. The preliminary work he of she does can save many headaches later.

Subdividing and developing real property requires attention to detail and working through many local regulatory obstacles. To manage these potentially long and costly processes, you must create an appropriate and efficient strategy to pursue development projects and approvals before actually filing paperwork.

One of the most important steps to take is to examine all existing permits and licenses to see if they are transferable. Often they are valuable to a buyer because they allow you certain land uses or operations. However, they may be treated as valuable by a seller, but will NOT be valuable to you because of your intended use of the site. Also, the permit could exist but not contain sufficient capacity to accommodate your planned expansion. For example, if you are planning to expand an industrial land use and the permit is already in place, does it allow for increased emissions and discharges? Does it address other ways the project adversely affects the environment? Studying the existing permit helps you decide whether to expand their capacity, or plan on investing in improvements that will make the property comply with existing regulations.

Search for new or newly proposed requirements. Regulatory compliance requirements may greatly affect your operating costs because of the cost of implementing new compliance measures. So things like daily discharges, operations emissions, or the method of required environmental steps can change your likelihood of making a profit. Learning about these measures before purchase can give you leverage in your negotiations.

Find all the most current versions of ordinances, applications, and checklists that are required in your locale. Many cities and counties have regulations for subdivisions and site review plans in place that allow for planned growth. You should acquaint yourself with the requirements long before filing a subdivision application or a site plan.

Locate any deed restrictions or covenants that could affect division of the land. Even if you create a project that is totally compliant with applicable regulations, you may still run into the problem of covenants and restrictions that exist in the deed affecting your use of the land. By taking this up with a qualified land use attorney, you can determine the effects of those restrictions on your project. It has been noted by several attorneys that planning officials often do not understand or correctly interpret the details of deed restrictions; an attorney can help you determine what they are to avoid expensive changes to your project.

When you have these regulations in hand, you and your project team should review them with your project in mind. Does your proposed development comply with applicable regulations? If not, how can you make it meet the technical specifications? If this preliminary review shows you that the proposed development may not conform to the applicable provision, can you adjust the proposal to avoid nonconformity? Can you make a waiver or variance request? Make a list of all the regulatory hurdles you may encounter and check them off as you deal with them. Every time you identify your own areas of noncompliance, you are saving yourself time and money.

Does your municipality allow for a pre-application review? Many localities give developers an opportunity for a review session in which you meet with the planning officials before engaging in a formal review process. This meeting affords you the opportunity to build a relationship with officials and the board. It also gives the planning officials an opportunity to identify the experts they may need to have on board to review your application, possibly speeding up your approval process.

About Current Use

The valuation of a land in current use is a frequent source of tension between developers and their municipalities. The question usually revolves around whether the valuation at the time the land use changes includes the value of any improvements on the land in question. Development plans, therefore, should include the notification to local assessors as soon as the land use change takes place.

If the project site has been classified as "current use" by the seller, there may be significant tax changes when you develop the parcel. For example, some states charge a land use change tax of 10 percent of the current market value. This charge is not triggered by a move on the part of the planning board, such as their approval of the project; it is triggered by your first construction or excavation efforts. To identify the tax liability you may have and to create a cost effective way of minimizing your change in use costs, consult with both legal and tax valuation advisers.

As part of due diligence, you will calculate all your development costs; those can be on-site as well as off-site, building and subdivision fees, overhead, refundable costs, and cost per lot.

If your due diligence process uncovers something odd (which is the entire purpose of the due diligence process), you as the purchaser will have some options. If the information that you obtain will make your investment undesirable and the problem cannot be resolved, you may need to withdraw from the deal.

If the due diligence information seems risky to lenders, they may withdraw their participation in the project. Lenders want to protect their investment, and they have plenty of other parties clamoring for their funds. Because the lenders are your partners in the development, you must keep their best interests in mind during planning.

The valuation of the building or land may also be changed based on new information. In the unlikely case the information is positive, the price rises.

Sometimes adverse information can be remedied by the seller before closing the deal. If there are liens, they can be paid; if there is a negative ESA report, steps can be taken to clean up the property or preserve wetlands or make other environmental alterations.

SITE EVALUATION CHECKLIST

Location
  Proximity to:
  ❑ Schools
  ❑ Churches
  ❑ Recreation
  ❑ Shopping and other key locations
  ❑ Police/Fire
  ❑ Major employers
  ❑ Airports
  ❑ Availability of transportation (all modes)
  ❑ Parking
  ❑ Road Frontage/visibility
  ❑ Size as compared to use

Topography and Hydrology:
  ❑ Elevation
  ❑ Slopes
  ❑ Swamp/marsh
  ❑ Drainage patterns
  ❑ Presence of toxic waste

Utilities in existence:
  ❑ Water
  ❑ Wells
  ❑ Sewer
  ❑ Cable TV
  ❑ Gas
  ❑ Electricity
  ❑ Telephone lines
  ❑ Street lights
  ❑ Storm sewers
  ❑ Trash collection

Buffered sources of:
- ❏ Floods
- ❏ Subsurface water
- ❏ Smoke
- ❏ Noxious odors
- ❏ Rail or highway traffic
- ❏ Any hazards or noise

Environmental impact of proposed site:
- ❏ Pollution
- ❏ Waste
- ❏ Noise
- ❏ Wildlife habitats, trees, parks

Market Trends

A market study is a vital part of the development process and one that cannot be overemphasized. A thorough market study minimizes your risk, improves your development plan, and helps your investors or lenders see that you are serious about your project. One of the most important parts of the study is examining the cyclical trends that are taking place in the economy and that have an effect on the industry.

Performing a market study involves local and national data. It is important to stay current on national trends because ultimately these changes trickle down to the local level, especially those that affect supply and demand. Changes in oil prices, unemployment and interest rates, and even the current amount of construction can all have an effect on your project. Large brokers like Cushman & Wakefield have statistics a developer needs, and it is also possible to find regional financial institutions and local brokers who keep current. Detailed data for the top 50 to 75 markets will be available on the Internet and can normally be obtained for a small fee.

Once you have a firm grasp of the current market, it is time to study the future market. The characteristics of demand are always dictated, at least in part, by changes in employment and population. Can you predict prospective rents? Absorption and vacancies? Can you calculate a perceived market value? Can you predict your operating expenses and net operating income?

THINGS TO CONSIDER WHEN DETERMINING DEMAND

1. **Always ask yourself why another developer has not already grabbed the opportunity**, especially if you are not a local developer. Examine the site and historical data. Talk to people close by, especially other business professionals. Ask the neighbors why they think the property has not sold. Although a good developer finds hidden opportunities, as a beginner you do not want to lose money.

2. **Know your competition.** Good marketing includes carefully identifying who your competition is and what real estate products they are creating. Compare the price and quality of their products to your own. Their sales will indicate your prospective sales. If your competitors are selling three units per month on the average, a new development probably will not sell much more than that.

3. **Consider your image.** The type of building you create sends a message to your clients, your future clients, investors and the general public. Functionality will dictate at least part of the design, but your image is created through your unique blend of design, style, and functionality.

Redevelopment or New Construction?

Your understanding of the market, your financing constraints, construction costs, and the cost of operation determine whether it would be easier to redevelop an existing piece of property rather than build from the ground up.

Class of Property

If you are considering renovations, it will be helpful to learn about the different building classifications. Properties are often classified according to a subjective division of buildings by desirability among tenants and investors. Criteria might include the age, location, construction quality, attractiveness of style, and level of maintenance The classes may be based on standards for market acceptance or the type of construction materials used. The following are some general standards of classifying properties, but they should by no means be used as the sole standard of measure.

CLASS A BUILDING

This building will generally show high quality and good design; the builder has used above-average materials, workmanship and finish. Investors and high quality tenants seek out a Class A building. It will be in excellent condition and very well managed, especially if the building is more than 10 years old.

CLASS B BUILDING

A building that is given the Class B designation is more utilitarian; it offers useful space but no special design characteristics. The layout and design are considered functional. The maintenance and management have been good. Typically, a Class B structure is 10 to 50 years old.

CLASS C BUILDING

Class C properties are typically older buildings without amenities. The maintenance and management are average at best, and they contain average to below average mechanical, electrical and ventilation systems. Generally, Class C structures attract moderate or low income tenants looking for affordable space.

There can be advantages to using an already existing property. For example, its market is established, so you will not have any surprise changes in the short term. Analyzing the market is easy, and you may be pleasantly surprised to learn that the area has attracted more people who will support your development. You may also find that the customer base has become more affluent since the original inception so that you can create a more upscale development.

Construction costs may be lower, and the turnaround may be faster with a preexisting development. The public usually is in agreement with projects that offer improvements to business properties. Also, you can build a good rapport with the public if you successfully revitalize a property that has significant nostalgic value.

In a developed site you will not have as much competition from others who want to enter the market—which almost guarantees your success.

If you have found a business or retail center that is under performing, you might do well with redevelopment; it is important that you first try to determine why it is not performing to its expected potential. Then consider these questions:

- Is the zoning agreeable with the design I have in mind?

- What parts of the design cannot be changed? How will those affect my ability to make something new and different?

- What will the tenants require to be involved in the change, or (if you do not want them to stay) move out entirely? You can buy out or remove tenants but both actions are costly.

- Can construction take place while the center remains in business? How will that work? What safety precautions will be required?

If you think the project is probably a go and the zoning does not have to be changed, you can save time, which translates into saving money. In fact, depending on the building's age, your plan may come under more flexible older restrictions and codes.

However, there are some downsides to redevelopment. Consider why the property is under performing. How easy is that to change? How attractive can you make the new layout, given the existence of the old one?

It is usually hard to estimate renovation costs, because there are so many unknowns in the equation. A new building can be a cookie cutter project, but a renovation requires adaptation at each step. Expenses can escalate greatly; someone who is new to the business will need to budget for plenty of unexpected costs.

Moving Forward

By now the research should have evolved into a clear-cut project design. If not, you may have decided that the site or design was not feasible and abandoned it. The whole purpose of the market study is to determine whether to continue forward with the plan. Although a market study usually costs 10 to 20 percent of your budget, it is much better to lose that amount now than the entire investment later. This is a difficult choice to make, especially for a beginning developer who is eager to get his or her feet wet, but being business savvy means knowing when to cut your losses.

Assuming that you have decided to move forward, it is now time to refine the idea through site selection, negotiation and creating a tentative project design. This is where you draw on the expertise of the team you have created (or are creating). Hiring the right team for project design is crucial. A strong design minimizes cost and risk and maximizes property use.

Refined Pro Forma

Now that you are getting into the real process, it is time to convert your draft pro forma to something more substantial. Using the same worksheets that you used before, you should now be in a better position to predict the year's income.

Flexibility is an absolute necessity in a business like real estate development, and one way to create a flexible budget is to set ranges of possible outcomes rather than absolute results. You would normally study the contingency plans for the input and output level in each of three categories: below normal (the worst case scenario), normal (the results that you expect), and above normal (the best case).

Management can also use pro forma statements for planning and control. During each fiscal period, management will evaluate the company's performance by comparing actual results to the pro forma projection. The statements are written in a columnar format so that it is easy to put them side by side to compare and analyze the possible results of different plans. Pro forma statements help managers perform ratio analyses, comparing projections against each other. They can examine variations that help them choose between budget alternatives.

4

Rules, Laws, and Playing Well With Others

No matter which kind of development you are interested in, restrictions placed on land use by zoning will determine the size and placement of the structures that are allowable on a given site. There will be front, side, and rear setbacks and access requirements. If your project is an industrial building or office development, you may have restrictions on building height and parking. There may also be landscaping and screening requirements. If you are not familiar with zoning regulations, you can learn the basics from a search on the Internet, by visiting the library, or by visiting the local zoning office to get a thorough understanding of which types of zoning are right for your use. For example, "R1-B" zoning is residential with a business. A building with this zoning is not one that you can rent out to a businessperson solely for their company. That would be in violation of the zoning ordinance.

Local government offices have information about restrictions that are pertinent to the area you are considering, as well as the type of development you will be doing. They can give insight into issues you may not have thought about yet. In fact, many real estate entrepreneurs visit zoning, building, and engineering on a regular basis. Developing relationships with these people can often lead to valuable information and potential deals.

Learning about competitors and government is easy for a local developer. You know who builds which type of development, who is considered successful, and who has a reputation for pushing their way through local government. You have some grasp already of what the market wants and which projects they have historically rejected. You understand the way local politics might affect the viability of your project. You may have an idea of the way the zoning board approaches new ideas.

If you do not already have a relationship with city officials, politicians, and the public, now is a good time to make friends with them. A successful developer creates projects from good ideas and answers to the human side of the market.

Density

When studying a potential site in terms of local laws, it is vital to examine the use and the permitted density of use for the zoning in place now. Analysis should be performed on the site based on the price per dwelling unit, rather than a price per square foot.

As an example, consider a three-acre site that allows 30 units per acre at a price of $690,000. This parcel yields a price per dwelling unit of $7,667. Now, compare that to a smaller 2.5-acre parcel that only allows 18 units per acre. At a sales price of $400,000, the smaller parcel yields a price per unit of $8,888, considerably higher than the first example, even though the parcel is smaller and costs less.

Unfortunately, you are more likely to find municipalities that resist your proposed plan than those who welcome a change. So when you are examining the current zoning for the tract you are considering, be sure to find out the zoning of the surrounding parcels. You also should take into consideration the possibility of changes to the zoning and how that will affect your project. If you are located in an area where the local government has been resistant to change, proceed slowly. Work cautiously and be prepared to spend time building positive relationships with the decision makers in the process. Developers must work within the existing rules and adhere to a legal process to facilitate change. Politics can offer you opportunities, or they can put up barriers that impede your project and, ultimately, affect your bottom line.

Let us take a look at some of the items that will affect your development efforts:

Neighborhood Statutes

If you are creating a subdivision or adding to an existing one, you will need to get a copy of the current neighborhood statutes. In fact, if the statutes have been in existence for a number of years it may be a good idea to obtain copies of older rules so that you can view them from a historical perspective. Even when considering raw land that lies outside the city and has never been subdivided, it is good to have a standard policy to search for statutes or neighborhood bylaws. Jurisdictions that lie just outside a city may have regulations because they may have been flagged for eventual annexation. These parcels may require changes in zoning or bylaws.

Approvals for both residential subdivisions and industrial parks usually require obtaining a building permit and platting the tract map. The site is then reviewed by the public before the final determination of restrictions.

Public Approvals

Public approvals are even more important than governmental approvals. Without the backing (or at least the grudging assent) of the public, your idea and your investment, can quickly evaporate.

Prepare for opposition and arguments from neighboring landowners and/or conservation groups. If you can anticipate the objections and have your argument ready, you will reduce the likelihood of their success. By creating a positive relationship early on with neighbors, conservationists and public officials, you will save yourself costly delays and possibly expensive changes to your project. The steps you have already taken if you are following this checklist will keep you organized through the permit process so that parties that are interested see the complete details of your proposed development. Their understanding can keep them from opposing you based on assumptions.

The public takes an active role in being sure that the environment is preserved and that they receive the type of product that benefits them. Their demands can cause a costly redesign or affect the ongoing operation of your project. The public sector affects every aspect of your venture, and because of this it is crucial that you or someone on your team maintains positive public relations.

Regulatory Issues for Office Buildings

As communities demand more discretion in response to the impact that an office development will have on their traffic, parking, and housing, the rules for developers become more complex. New regulations in the past 20 years were created to control negative impact and raise tax revenues. Office developments usually have a positive effect on tax revenue; however, they generate less revenue than, say, a retail development and the potential sales tax source there. Many cities have chosen to tie office development with public projects, for example requiring developers to build up to 200 units of low-income housing for every one million square feet of office space they construct.[ii] Developers have been asked to add streets, contribute to highways or acceleration/ deceleration lanes, and numerous other traffic improvements. Off-site infrastructure requirements from local government can be costly in terms of both money and time.

The physical characteristics of your chosen site can make or break your overall plan. The buildable square footage may be lessened if the shape is long and narrow, if part of it is in a flood plain, or if most of the land will not pass the soils test.

Soils must pass tests to show their load-bearing capacity, but the capacity strictly from a test is not a given. Information can be obtained from other local brokers or builders or from geologists and soil engineers to gain insight into the details of the soil.

The feasibility of the project layout may be a concern before you purchase a site if the layout appears to be difficult. Most developers at this stage have to hire consultants to determine soil load-bearing capacity and drainage runoff.

At this time you also should investigate the possibility of hazardous wastes. It is the responsibility of the owner to remove any known hazardous wastes from a property, so if your contract does not have a clause to remove wastes, the costs will fall to you.

Some local agencies require an archaeological survey to be made. If artifacts are discovered on your property, the subsequent excavation can delay construction for months. If this is required in your area, you may consider making the purchase contract contingent on the satisfactory completion of the survey.

Environmental Issues

Environmental sensitivity has affected nearly every level of the real estate development process, leading to open-space requirements, restrictions on building in wetlands or canyons, and lower density allowances. These changes have reduced the overall amount of land that is available for development, and they have reduced the permissible uses for the land that is available.

It is a creative challenge for a developer to meet the environmental and conservation factors. Developers can respond to these demands by protecting the environment and enhancing it with richly planted areas that promote clean air and reduce noise, structures to prevent erosion of sloping areas, and by creating homeowner associations to maintain the environment in the future.

Wetlands

Wetlands refer to any type of water, whether it is a lake, a stream, marsh, bog, or other similar area. Under U.S. law, a permit from the Army Corps of Engineers is required before you can dredge or fill wetlands areas. The purpose of the permit requirement is to protect wetlands from destruction and harm, so one of the first things you want to do as a developer if you see any water on the site is conduct a floodplain study. Wetlands used to be considered wasted space, but we have learned that they not only provide habitats for fish and other wildlife, but they also help to collect floodwaters and improve water quality. This gives them value both economically and environmentally.

By protecting and restoring wetlands, developers ensure the health of our watershed. Even wetlands that have been filled and drained can be restored to their natural function and value. Wetlands fall under the jurisdiction of the Environmental Protection Agency (EPA), the Army Corps of Engineers, and the U.S. Fish and Wildlife Service.

ADDITIONAL TIP

Learn where your local floodplains are by obtaining a flood hazard boundary map from the Federal Emergency Management Agency **www.fema.gov**. If land is within the 100-year floodplain, it may be developable subject to certain restrictions.

Hazardous Wastes

In the 1980s, laws were passed that required the investigation and cleanup of sites that were contaminated with hazardous waste products. These laws impose the liability on owners, lessors, lessees, and others who manage or purchase the contaminated properties, even if you are unaware at the time of lease or purchase of the contamination.

A hazardous substance, under the Model Toxics Control act, can be any chemical or waste that threatens the health of humans or the environment.

A thorough environmental site assessment should consist of a physical site inspection including soil and water sampling, a comprehensive records review, and a site history. The consultant can obtain much of the information from federal, state, and local regulatory agencies, but they will probably conduct other interviews as well.

Potential Environmental Exposures

- Historical industrial use of property

- Contamination from adjacent properties

- Local or regional soil or groundwater contamination

- Air emissions from ammonia-based refrigeration systems

- Hazardous chemical storage

- On-site garbage incinerator

- Sick building syndrome from many causes such as carbon monoxide, bacterial air releases from carpet fumes, and faulty heating, ventilation, or air conditioning systems

- Construction debris

- Lack of proper containment of hazardous materials at loading and unloading sites

- Inadequate hazardous waste management

- Buried tree stumps and construction debris

- Past on-site waste disposal practices

- On-site sanitary septic system or undersized packaged wastewater treatment plant

- Past and present septic systems

- "Midnight dumping" or improper disposal of wastes in dumpsters

- Spillage/stained soils

- Surface water runoff

- Unknown past manufacturing operations at the site

- Floor drain discharge path that drains directly to the ground

- Unknown hazardous material usage by tenant(s)

- Poor or nonexistent management of underground tanks and piping

- Historical underground or above ground fuel storage tanks

- Improperly maintained PCB-containing electrical equipment

- Businesses that are known to generate hazardous wastes such as dry cleaners, medical facilities, photo developers, and printers

- Businesses that have the potential to have a chemical release to the ground or sewer such as restaurants, hardware and paint stores, bakeries, gas stations, and plant nurseries

- Use of chemicals at multiple locations on a property

- Silt in nearby streams from improper erosion control management

Some Environmental Contaminants

- Medical waste from doctor and/or dentist offices

- Dry cleaning solvents

- Pesticides

- Herbicides

- Construction debris

- Paint thinners and paint cans

- Cleaning solvents, degreasers, tar, and glues

- Petroleum like gasoline, diesel, fuel oils, and waste oils

- Lead

- Asbestos

- PCBs and radioactive material

- Formaldehyde

- Radon

Phase I Environmental Site Assessment

The Phase I Environmental Site Assessment should be considered standard in any real estate transaction. This is required by the Comprehensive Environmental Response, Compensation, and Liability Act (CERCLA) which imposes very strict liability on the "potentially responsible party" (PRP), who may be required to clean up contamination due to the release of hazardous substances into the ground or water. PRPs can be property owners who do not exercise due diligence and face expensive clean-up liability even though it was pre-existing. That is why, over the past 20 years, the ESA process and due diligence have evolved. Finding out that hazardous substances exist on the property allows the buyer to choose whether to walk away or negotiate with the seller for clean-up.

CERCLA does not provide guidelines for conducting an appropriate inquiry into the property's history, so industry groups such as the American Society of Testing and Material (ASTM) have developed the standards. In 2002, the EPA was required to establish standards for all appropriate inquiries under the Federal Small Business Liability Relief and Brownsfields Revitalization Act. More recently, the EPA made some changes to the way Phase I ESA is conducted, which we will cover briefly here.

WHAT CAN I EXPECT DURING A PHASE I ASSESSMENT?

Typically, the Phase I will consist of any or all of the following:

- A historical review of the property's use and improvements.

- A review of building, zoning, planning and other records on the property and the adjacent parcels.

- An inspection of all buildings for the presence of asbestos containing materials.

- A review of the sewer, water and state/federal environmental agency records and files on the property and adjacent parcels.

- A review of any reports that have been filed under CERCLA or other statutes concerning environmental conditions. (This includes events like releases or threatened releases on the property and adjacent parcels).

- A visual inspection of the property and all improvements.

- Verification of past owners' and tenants' storage, creation, or discharge of hazardous materials and/or wastes.

- A review of appropriate safeguards about procedures with respect to hazardous substances on the property (permits, notices).

- Examination for the presence of wetlands and radon.

- Analysis of aerial photographs, both past and present that show the existence of ponds, disposal areas, and the construction and destruction of buildings over time.

- Interviews with neighbors of the property.

On November 1, 2006, the EPA set forth a new rule on All Appropriate Inquiries (AAI). The AAI rules are designed to outline how prospective property purchasers can satisfy their due diligence obligations when they purchase either developed or undeveloped property. For the most part, the new rule does not make huge changes to the way that people have been conducting a Phase I Environmental Site Assessment (ESA). But the subtleties of the law make it especially important to follow the changes.

Before the EPA instigated the new AAI rule, prospective purchasers simply hired an Environmental Professional (EP) to perform an ESA, which from 1997 to November 2006 conformed to the American Society for Testing and Materials' (ASTM) Phase I Environmental Site Assessment process. After announcing the change in 2005, ASTM issued a new standard, ASTM 1527-05, which conforms to the new AAI rule. The changes that are evident in the AAI and the ASTM 1527-05 standards impact the following vital components of the ESA process:

- The interviewing process

- The time to review historical sources

- Gaps in data

- Life of validity of the Phase I ESA

- Minimum experience and/or educational requirements

- New requirements imposed on the prospective purchaser

BASIC CHANGES FROM PREVIOUS RULINGS

The interviewing process for the EP is now mandatory; he or she must interview current owners or occupants of the property. The EP must interview one or more of the following: current and past managers of the facility; past owners, occupants and operators of the property; or employees of current and past occupants of the property if they are likely to have material information about environmental releases. Finally, the EP must interview neighboring (or nearby) property owners or occupants. Under the prior ruling, interviewing these individuals was suggested but was not required

Under the old rule, the EP was required to evaluate and analyze uses of the property from the present all the way back to the property's first obvious use, or to 1940, whichever was earlier. Under the new rule, there is not a formal date requirement written; instead, it says the EP must search as far back as "it can be shown that the property contains structures or from the time the property was first used for residential, agricultural, commercial, industrial, or governmental purpose."

The EP must also identify in the ESA report all data gaps and discuss whether those data gaps affected his or her ability to identify recognized environmental conditions. He/she must also identify on record all the sources of information that were consulted with and address data gaps.

The new rule has changed the length of validity of the Phase I ESA prepared by the EP. In the past, a Phase I ESA less than 180 days old was allowed as valid. The new rule changes this limit to one year and certain information like regulatory records reviews, on-site visits, personal interviews, and environmental liens are required to be updated if the information is more than six months old.

Under the new rule, the EP must hold a professional engineer license or certification, a professional geologist license or certification, or hold another state or federal government certification or an environmental professional license. He must have three years of relevant full-time experience as an environmental professional. Alternatively, he can have a degree in science or engineering and five years of relevant full-time experience, or have no degree in these particular fields but 10 years of relevant full-time experience.

Finally, the new rule requires that the EP and/or purchaser (and user of any ESA) evaluate the purchaser's specialized knowledge of the subject property or other reasonably ascertainable information about the property. It asks the prospective purchaser to compare the fair market value of the property as an uncontaminated parcel to the contemplated purchase price to evaluate whether the proposed purchase price reflects potential environmental conditions that require further evaluation.

Phase II Environmental Site Assessment

Whereas a Phase I assessment determines the likelihood that hazardous wastes are present, the objective of the Phase II Environmental Site Assessment is to evaluate the nature and extent of the contamination and to determine how much contamination there is in relation to the threshold. The assessment will involve working with the appropriate regulatory agency for sampling and reporting purposes. Typically, Phase II involves preparation of site safety plans and work plans, site assessment, periodic monitoring and risk assessment. It may also include an evaluation of the risk-based cleanup levels, although every site is different so the approach to the sampling program can vary.

Groundwater and soil samples, which are not taken in Phase I, are part of Phase II testing. The tests will also identify whether the source of contamination is a point source, or non-point; whether the type of contaminant is volatile; whether it affects the soil, groundwater, or both; how deep the contamination goes; and the depth to groundwater.

During Phase II, the levels of contamination are compared to a general cleanup standard, called threshold action levels. If the levels of contaminants that are present are below these general standards, you may not be required to clean up the site. If there is no listed standard for the contaminant, the risk can be analyzed to determine the significance of contamination.

To avoid any liability by a previous landowner, the PRP has to conduct all appropriate inquiry. This enables you to rely on the "innocent landowner defense" if a hazardous substance is ever found on the property.

You may hear properties referred to as "Brownsfields." These are sites that are suspected of contamination because of something in their industrial history. Whether the contamination is present, buyers fear liability due to the preexisting condition, so redevelopment is hindered. Therefore, many Brownsfields are idle. The federal government, along with some states and environmental authorities, has created programs to locate distressed properties and provide funding assistance.

Defining the Need for Environmental Insurance

Renovation, demolition, and construction of commercial properties can create many potential environmental exposures. Commercial properties can become environmental liabilities due to the potential of past usage or poor building practices, as well as inadequate waste management or housekeeping by builders and/or tenants. Federal law allows the recovery of at least some costs by everyone who is associated with the contaminated property. So in addition to the loss of property value and the loss of future business, the recovery can cost a developer millions of dollars.

EXAMPLES

- **Previous illegal dumping or burial of hazardous materials** can result in soil or groundwater contamination.

- **Pollution from neighboring properties** may cause soil, surface water, or groundwater contamination.

- **Municipal sewer pipes can become corroded from solvents or other hazardous wastes** which are illegally poured down sewer drains; they result in groundwater and soil contamination.

- **Sewer lines can constrict or clog** because of poorly maintained or absent grease traps from businesses like bakeries and restaurants.

- **Outdoor spilling of pesticides, paints, solvents, flammable solvents, fertilizers**, and other products from hardware stores can cause soil, surface, or groundwater contamination.

- **Solvents, thinners, epoxy, and paint that are improperly thrown away** into a dumpster can contaminate landfills, which leach into the surrounding soil and groundwater.

- **Spills or leaks of hazardous material at loading docks or roadways** can result in soil and surface water contamination and sewer and storm drain impairment.

- **Residual contamination from fertilizers or pesticides** from past farming operations can contaminate soil and groundwater.

- **Old, abandoned wells that are not properly closed** serve as an open conduit for groundwater contamination.

- **Improper management of protected or sensitive areas** such as wetlands can cause soil and groundwater pollution.

Environmental Liability Issues

Is there a threat of financial responsibility when commercial real estate developers are in full compliance with environmental regulations?

When a building contractor recently cleared a construction site for a new shopping mall, he hauled the construction debris to the local landfill, as was customary. The municipality discovered that the debris contained hazardous materials, which were dumped illegally. They sued the developer for clean-up costs, which the court assessed at more than $1 million.

A well-known excavation company was digging a foundation hole when an underground oil storage tank that no one knew existed was ruptured, spilling hundreds of gallons before the rupture was sealed off. In the meantime, streets and adjacent properties were covered. The developer was sued for personal bodily injury, property damage, and he paid for clean-up. Total costs were estimated to be in excess of $5 million.

A business is liable for any environmental contamination that originates from site- or activity-related business operations. So when developers hired licensed third-party vendors to transport, store, treat, and dispose of potentially hazardous materials, they took on the risk; it does not automatically transfer to the third-party vendor. Contractors and subcontractors hired to work at a facility or to provide a client service present environmental and financial risk to you as a developer.

To minimize exposure, you should carefully verify each vendor's qualifications and study their compliance with state and federal licensing and regulations governing hazardous materials. Creating a work contract that legally transfers liability to the vendor can help further reduce exposure, but even when you take all these precautions, the bottom line is that you are still at risk. If an environmental accident happens and the vendor cannot cover the clean-up and third-party compensation costs, you as the developer will be held responsible for the leftover costs.

What Does Environmental Insurance Offer?

Study the environmental insurance that is available. It can actually help to push your purchase toward closing. The insurance market can give you a variety of risk management tools, all of which are cost effective. Environmental insurance can be very useful in addressing the liability risks you uncover during due diligence. A qualified environmental insurance broker will provide you with information on insurance policies, premiums, and a variety of terms and conditions that can help your transaction reach closing. Policies cover losses due to on and off-site pollution, transportation, and disposal sites. They can even cover third-party claims due to pollution that causes bodily injury, property damage, and/or cleanup.

As a purchaser, you might not know the extent of environmental problems up front. Until you meet with state or federal authorities, and possibly perform further tests, you will not know what you are up against. This is a good time to present a contract with a contingency clause. It might put a limit on the amount that you will spend performing clean-up. You would word it along the lines of:

The purchase is dependent upon confirmation that the required environmental waste removal can be completed for less than $350,000.

Green Building

The concept of "green building" (building with a sensitivity to environmental issues) is growing by leaps and bounds. In fact, Boston became the first city in the United States to create a set of green building standards that will be required of all new private development in the city. The standards cover all projects that are over 50,000 square feet, and are slated to become part of the municipal zoning laws.

The goal of green building is to make projects both environmentally friendly and energy efficient. The standards in Boston cover the methods of waste material disposal and energy efficiency ratings of walls and glass. City officials will be responsible for the confirmation that developers have met the requirements. For a new developer, green building may be a viable way to distinguish oneself from the competition.

Smart Growth

People dislike urban sprawl as it has a harmful long-term effect on their cities, towns, rural communities, and ultimately their environmental landscape. They feel that the long commutes cost time and money, create pollution and do not foster a sense of place.

Couple that knowledge with a strong environmental ethic, and you have the basis for what has come to be known as "smart growth" that encourages a compact development with an efficient use of the land and preserved open space. It is a mixed use development that allows more destinations within the grasp of people who want to walk, bicycle, or make a short trip. It is a type of development that, rather than enjoying the short-term profits realized from creating a large rental unit in the country, is created closer to the city's center to allow residents shorter commutes and less pollution.

One of the most important components of smart growth is that it focuses on preserving open space and habitat, reusing land in a productive, eco-friendly way, and it protects existing water supplies and air quality.

Smart growth encourages social and recreational activities and the use of local transportation systems. It affects where schools and major highways are built. At the same time, it restores community and vitality to the cities and towns, centering activity there.

Homeowners want to live in nice neighborhoods and communities. They want good schools, easy access to parks and recreational areas, a short drive to shopping areas. Studies show that people want communities that resemble pre-World War II towns with an active town center and higher density than many developers are offering.

Higher density does not cause high crime rates, contrary to popular belief; in fact, with communities that are designed with diverse housing types and densities, and a varied population with differing ages, incomes, and cultures, crime rates actually drop.

Smart growth is not a cookie cutter principle; you cannot enter a community and dictate how it should grow. Rather, you will have to study the community's sense of place to get a feel for their emphasis. What are they looking for? How can you fill that niche?

They may simply need to improve the housing options available to them, which can be accomplished with infill development rather than sprawl. They may want a town center to give them access to shopping and activities while reducing their daily transportation time. By learning what the community is looking for, you will create a product that not only fills a need now, but one that has the chance for staying power.

Components of a Smart Growth Community

MIX OF HOUSING TYPES

One of the main components of community growth is the type of housing that it offers. With smart growth, the strategy is to construct housing for people of varying income levels. By giving the residents a range of housing choices, communities can actually limit the effect that developing has on the environment. They can work to balance housing with available jobs and create access to commercial enterprises. Best of all, people from all income levels will be present in the resulting development.

WALKABLE COMMUNITIES

A walkable community is one that has an easy, safe pedestrian commute to other homes, offices, stores, transportation, and schools. This type of community is designed to accommodate foot traffic, bicyclists, transit riders, and vehicles. This increases the choices of transportation residents can use, but it must be created in a way that fosters safety and invites pedestrian channels.

Traditionally, land use regulations have prohibited mixed-use developments. By segmenting the design, government agencies actually limited accessibility by pedestrians, making walking less attractive while causing more miles in automobile travel.

Biking and walking instead of driving can save fuel, reduce emissions and care maintenance, and encourage residents to live a healthier lifestyle. Compact development and mixed use actually can help reduce the number of miles driven up to 30 percent.

To do these things, the development must first have access to commercial and economic centers, neighbors, or other recreational activities that people would want to travel to. If they are not already in place, improvements like a bike trail system, bike lanes on streets, bike parking, pedestrian crossings, and pedestrian paths (or trails or sidewalks) can be added to the master plan.

USE OF PUBLIC TRANSPORTATION

Studies have found that mixed-use/compact neighborhoods

tend to use transit at all times of the day. Smart growth includes locating new developments within a reasonable distance of as many types of public transportation as possible.

PRESERVATION OF OPEN SPACE

Open space, in the smart growth sense, means the natural areas surrounding the community. They may be recreational, habitats for plants and animals, farm or ranch lands. They could simply be areas of natural beauty. They could be "preserved" areas like wetlands.

Open space preservation protects all of these while providing significant improvement to the quality of the environment and water as well as minimizing air and noise pollution. It maintains natural beauty, controls wind and controls erosion.

To encourage open space preservation, some cities participate in activities like the Cities for Climate Protection campaign, **http://www.iclei.org**, which asks them to "adopt policies and implement reductions in local greenhouse gas emissions, improve air quality, and enhance urban livability and sustainability."

Although smart growth has its critics, it can be more profitable for you as a developer. Managed growth is better for the environment as well as more cost-efficient for local government. All in all, managed growth over the next half century should prove to have a positive effect.

Become Involved in Smart Growth

Many developers these days approach the city for information. Town councils always have plans for growth. They will not give you an opinion of which way they want your work to go, but they know how they want the physical growth to manifest itself. What they will do is tell you the details of their plans, including the utilities, roads, and so on. These are of special importance to you because they are so costly; your first project would be best created in an area where there are existing utilities that can handle the growth you will create, if at all possible. So if you acquire raw land, you want to be within the boundaries the local government has laid out.

5

Your First Development

One of the best ways to protect your business and its assets, as well as your good name, is through learning everything you can about contracts and contract law. This is not to take the place of the advice of a good attorney; however, it is savvy to be aware of the various components of contracts and deeds, and to be familiar with contractual language.

As you pick your first location, try to minimize your costs through the use of proper purchase contract tools. For example, rather than purchasing the property outright, consider the situations in which you would not develop the land or building. You might ask for an option to purchase, making it contingent upon receiving the appropriate financing, marketing, or the design feasibility. Note that "contingent" is not the same thing as "subject to;" minor details like this will make or break your profit margin, so this is a good time to employ an attorney who is familiar with commercial real estate contracts.

Contracts 101

About the Deed

The legal, signed document conveying the title of a piece of property from one person to another is called the deed. There are several types of deeds; here we will discuss three of them:

A **Warranty Deed** conveys the warranty that the grantor (the person conveying the property) is conveying ownership exactly as described in the legal description of the deed. He warrants, or promises, to stand behind the title, not only back to the date that he purchased it, but all the way to the origin of the property. If there is a problem in the future, the purchaser may sue the grantor for breach of warranty.

A **Bargain and Sale Deed** warrants the integrity of the title only from the date that the grantor took ownership. It does not guarantee that the property is free of liens or encumbrances, although the grantor may choose to add such guarantees to the deed.

A **Quitclaim Deed** tells you that the grantor is making no representation or warranty about the deed to you; he is only conveying to you what he owns (whatever that may be). In fact, he is not professing that his claim to the property was valid. Quitclaim deeds are often used to convey property from one spouse to another. They also may be used as gifts or to remove cloud on a title. You should note that in some jurisdictions, a quitclaim deed may not prove that you are the bona fide purchaser; further proof may be necessary to obtain title.

FOR A DEED TO BE VALID, IT NEEDS TO MEET FIVE BASIC CRITERIA:

1. The deed must be in writing and must contain a legal description sufficient to describe the piece of property that is being conveyed.

2. The grantor must have the legal right to grant the privilege or rights, and language to that effect must be used in the deed ["I, (NAME), hereby grant to (NAME)"].

3. The parties must be legally competent and capable to receive the title.

4. A seal must be affixed to it (acknowledged before a notary public or a civil law notary) and it must be signed by all parties.

5. It must be delivered to, and accepted by, the grantee (signed, sealed, delivered).

ADDITIONAL TIP

It is not required that you record the deed; however, to avoid future claims on the title, you should record the deed as soon after closing as you possibly can.

The real estate purchase contract is one of the most important documents involved in your transaction. It is the legal document that outlines your terms of purchase, due diligence, and what will happen if the deal does not come to fruition.

OPTION AGREEMENT

An option agreement is a type of real estate contract with an obligation on the seller's part to sell. The buyer, under an option agreement, may lose the deposit if he decides to terminate the deal, but the seller will not be able to sue the purchaser for breach of contract.

The deposit on an option agreement will usually be at least 5 percent of the selling price. The deposit will go to the seller regardless of whether the deal comes to fruition.

A typical real estate contract is normally measured in months; an option agreement will last longer, maybe even two years. Often the agreed selling price will be higher than the property value as it stands. You might consider adding a clause that you (the purchaser) can choose to close early with 30 days' written notice. That way, if your plans move forward quickly, you are able to obtain the property early.

An option agreement is good for you as a new developer because it gives you time to determine whether the property works for you; for example, you can purchase land under an option agreement and attempt to get it rezoned. Tying up the property gives you time to get a public hearing and then fight any appeals that might arise.

ADDITIONAL TIP

Be sure that the seller agrees to cooperate in every way if you are attempting to rezone a property — including attending public hearings about the rezoning.

Often instead of an option agreement, you will enter into a contract with contingencies. In this case, the completion of the terms of the contract are contingent upon your obtaining something (in the above case, rezoning). If you are unable to get the rezoning, then you may terminate the contract. In this case the seller will return the down payment to you, assuming that is what your contract says.

Contingency contracts are also useful when you are trying to purchase several adjoining parcels of land to create a larger development, or if you are only willing to accept financial risk up to a certain point.

In a contingency contract, you have tied up the property with no money at risk, because you will get your money back if things do not go as planned.

PROMISSORY NOTES

A promissory note is an unconditional promise to pay a certain amount of money to the lender. The note must include the time the funds are due to be paid, or state that the payment is on demand. The note maker promises to pay a certain amount of money at that time. The notes may be one of several types:

- **Straight** – the terms call for payment of interest during the term of the note, with the principal due and payable on a particular date.

- **Installment note** - periodic payment, with the principal payments separate from the interest payments.

- Installment note with periodic payments of fixed amounts (amortized payments) that contain both interest and principal.

- **Adjustable rate** - interest rate that varies dependent upon an index, usually the CPI.

- A demand note that becomes due when the holder makes demand for it.

To be legal, your promissory note should:

- Be signed by the note maker.

- Contain an unconditional promise to pay a sum in money, with no other promise, order, or obligation given by the note maker.

- Payable on demand OR at a particular time.

- Payable to the bearer.

Levels of Risk

As you start your development, people may advise you to stay within the boundaries of the market. But where are those boundaries? And is this always the best advice?

To know where the boundaries are, be sure that you estimate future demand; do not work from the standpoint of today's market as consultants see it.

Know who you are. Does your risk profile withstand the competition from other projects that are targeted to the same market? If you are bidding against numerous other people—all of whom have more money, more political connections, and more staff than you—it may be time to reconsider your position. Rather than acting like a big developer, this may be the time to rethink your projections toward a more modest goal.

Since development is a process that repeats, each step brings in more risk. There is no way to avoid having your investment at risk. All you can do is limit the total amount of loss you might suffer through this one project. You will do that by analyzing each step, determining where the risk factors are, and trying to build in safeguards.

Land development is probably the highest risk for beginning business owners. If you are developing land, you will get pre-commitment letters from builders before approaching lenders. The letters themselves do not guarantee that you will sell the lots; a guarantee is available, though, if the letters are backed by letters of credit. A letter of credit guarantees that the builder's bank will pay the balance on the lots.

As a beginning developer, you cannot eliminate liability, but you can probably limit it to a certain amount. It is normal for an institutional investor to try to shift the risk to you; you need to try to shift it back in the other direction. Knowing the ins and outs of the contracts and clauses involved in your profession will help you limit your risk.

A dead deal, for example, involving an acquisition that does not go through, can cost you money. Many investors require that the developer pay 65 percent to 75 percent of the dead deal cost. This will be addressed in a clause of your contract; be sure to understand what you are signing!

Limiting Risk through Contractual Language

We have addressed option agreements. However, you can also limit your risk through mortgage contingencies and clauses in your contracts.

A contingency is an obligation that must be met for a contract to be performed (completed). Contingencies are often present in contracts to purchase. They can suspend the contract until certain events occur, or they can cause the contract to be cancelled if a problematic event occurs.

You might make the purchase of a property contingent upon obtaining a loan for the property. That means if you cannot secure appropriate financing, you are not obligated to buy; usually the contract allows you to receive a refund on the entire down payment in this case.

Sample Clause from a Purchase Contract

Purchaser's obligations under this Agreement are contingent upon Purchaser obtaining and successfully closing upon mortgage financing for the acquisition of the Property from a lender satisfactory to Purchaser and in an amount and upon such other terms and conditions as Purchaser deems acceptable within sixty (60) days after date of this Contract.

As you can see, you would be able to walk away from this contract if you were not able to obtain the funding. Other contingencies could be a successful inspection, a satisfactory soil test, or even acquiring a different piece of property.

A zoning contingency can be useful to tie up a piece of land or other property so that you can walk the property through the rezoning process. With the right wording, you can tie up the property with no time limit, and with little or no money at risk.

Sample Zoning Contingency

Buyer, at buyer's expense, will make a formal written application for zoning approval, variance, non-conforming use, or special exception from (municipality:)_____to use the property as: _____. If final, unappealable approval is not obtained, buyer will:

(A) Accept the property and its current zoning; or

(B) Terminate the contract by means of written notice to the Seller, with all deposit monies to be returned to the Buyer in accordance with the terms of the Agreement of Sale; or

(C) Enter into a mutually acceptable written agreement with Seller.

Dig a little deeper: Normally the seller will want protection for himself under the contract as well. So in the first purchase contract, the wording might be:

This contract is contingent upon Purchaser obtaining a "loan." Purchaser agrees to make immediate application for the mortgage financing, will prosecute same with diligence, and do all things in its power to obtain the mortgage in question. If buyer does not obtain financing after application to at least three lenders, Seller may terminate this contract and refund the deposit.

One successful developer described his job as "an interesting journey. It is a learning process. You have to be persistent and you have to be a problem solver; it is like you are trying to put together a 10,000-piece jigsaw puzzle, but nobody's cut the pieces out. So you are creating it yourself."

There are plenty of purchase contracts available through your local MLS or even your lender. Some sample contracts can be found on the companion CD-ROM.

Land Development

The process of developing raw land is one of the foremost challenges in the real estate market today. A developer can turn a tract of land into a profitable, marketable development that is residential, commercial, or industrial — or a mix.

Developers must choose the site, determine the needs of the project, and plan the layout. Before the actual construction takes place, the developer must perform a cost analysis and prepare the financing. He then contracts for the actual creation of physical structures, and supervises the construction. Finally, he sells or leases the finished product to the market for which it was planned.

Subdivision is the process of taking both physical and legal steps to convert raw land into developed land.[ii] Over decades, subdivision regulations have been created by local governments, and all developers must be aware of these restrictions and follow them closely. These regulations involve streets, utilities, easements and setbacks, and they vary from one municipality to the next. Regulations also dictate land use (residential, agricultural, retail, industrial) and zoning.

Zoning is a second level description of land use; it gives the exact detail of how a property can be used. Typically, zoning districts regulate the size and number of buildings, the distance from the building to streets and lot lines, the amount of parking, and possibly the size and placement of signage.

If the property you have got your eye on does not have the appropriate zoning, you must apply to have it rezoned, a long-term, possibly arduous process involving public resistance. Before purchasing a parcel of land, you need to determine the likelihood that the change will be allowed, and that it is worth the time, energy, and financial investment required.

Even when you do have the approved zoning, your rights to develop may be limited by nearby residents or by the political atmosphere of the area. Clearly, land development is quite risky, but it can be extremely profitable as long as you have the resources in place to withstand a long investment period without a positive cash flow.

Although the initial steps (and terminology) vary from state to state, the first step of purchasing property will be drawing up the purchase contract. This document outlines all the terms of the purchase: the price, due diligence, responsibilities for title and other documents, and it names the actions that will be taken in the event that the sale does not go through. Because this is your first development, it is important to keep your purchase contract as simple as possible; it is always best to use an attorney, no matter how simple the paperwork appears to be.

In 1968, Congress enacted the Interstate Land Sales Full Disclosure Act, created to protect consumers from fraud in the purchase or lease of land. It somewhat follows the structure of the Securities Law of 1933. Developers who are creating subdivisions of 100 or more non-exempt lots must register with HUD and provide every purchaser with a Property Report. This report gives relevant information about the subdivision and must be in the purchaser's hands before signing any contract or agreement.

What does this mean for you? If you are creating a residential subdivision, you should file the general subdivision registration with the attorney general's office before starting construction. Your attorney will be able to determine whether your project falls under these requirements and can prepare the necessary documents to register you or exempt you from registration under this Act.

Tips for a Successful Land Purchase

- Get your own appraisals. Do not depend on appraisals that are not thorough enough to address hazardous or unacceptable conditions of the land.

- Write the purchase contract in a way that makes the seller supportive of your efforts.

- Ask the seller to allow you to obtain a conditional use permit (if it is required) during the escrow period.

- If the seller is financing the property, put a clause in the contract stating that some of the land is available to begin construction.

- Read all the fine print.

- Use a title company that will back you if you need it; some of the nationwide companies enfranchise local offices separately from the national chain.

(This list adapted from Professional Real Estate Development, 2nd edition, Peiser and Frej 2003.

Contingencies in contracts were outlined in the first part of this chapter. They are the steps that precede the purchase. You may make the sale subject to obtaining financing, or subject to feasibility studies like soils, title, and site planning. These are contingencies that allow a buyer to back out of a contract without losing his deposit.

One important contingency on land that requires rezoning is that the seller will support you through the process. Some developers take this a step further and make the purchase price based on the number of allowable building units. This encourages your seller to back you on obtaining approval for higher densities.

After you have gone through the zoning approval process, it is time to develop the site plan that is drawn up with the assistance of an architect, an engineer, a land planner, and possibly a landscape architect. The site plan is designed with careful attention to compliance with the local zoning rules and regulations. It will show where you plan to locate the buildings and parking and how you will hook into the utilities. Site plans are fairly concrete, and only a minor change can take place without re-initiating the approval process. You will need to check with your jurisdiction on the term of your site plan; some are valid forever, but some expire after only one year.

Platting is the name for the subdivision of land into smaller sections. Cities and counties set standards for the lot descriptions to be entered into their records, so you need to describe the land in a way that conforms to their system. When you have subdivided the land, you will submit a plat showing the local government your individual blocks and lots. Doing so may require a public hearing, depending on the region and local statutes.

Zoning Checklist

Does your plat fit within the:

- Restrictive covenants already in place?

- The required open space?

- Street width?

- Street length?

- Alleys?

- Lot size (including total area as well as width and depth)?

- Setbacks (street to the house; house to the lot line)?

- Number of units per acre?

- Minimum size of units?

In addition to fitting into the zoning criteria of your proposed development, there is one subjective question: does the new development fit with the neighborhood? To answer this question, you need to study the design of the surrounding developments, particularly the lot sizes, setbacks, garage placements and the overall feel. You do not want to build townhouses with parking lots if the surrounding ones have garages underneath. You do not want to construct a PUD (planned unit) development in the middle of horse country. These innovative ideas have probably worked somewhere, for somebody, but remember: This is your first development, and if your "big idea" is to succeed, save the innovation for later!

The most important part of the plan for you as a developer is figuring out how much of the land is developable. You must subtract out any amount that contains floodplains or other unbuildable features, easements, or right-of-way frontage. The part that is left must be scrutinized carefully to perform yet another financial analysis.

Your site planner will help you with a preliminary diagram of the site's topographical and other relevant features. Then he will make several layouts of how your roads, lots, and open spaces will work together. You will take this plan and study every detail:

- Do the traffic patterns work?

- How is the access in and out of the neighborhood?

- Do the views from the windows honor the owner's privacy?

- Are you making the best use of natural land features that are in place?

A final map will eventually be drawn, after much input from your entire team that will include the site planner, contractor, civil engineer and other key staff players. You may also select a political consultant or public representative.

The site map is drawn to scale with one inch equal to 500 feet. Besides the obvious land use requirements, the site map should include the existing zoning of surrounding areas and any boundary lines for districts like schools and police.

Where to Get Your Site Information

The original base map that you work from is created from geological maps, zoning maps, and aerial photos. Where do you find all this information?

- For **geological maps**, you can turn to local sources or the U.S. Geological Survey and/or the U.S. Department of Agriculture.

- **Zoning maps** are available for purchase from your city zoning department.

- **Aerial photos** are available from private companies.

- **Topographic maps** and other environmental assessments are found at one or several of the following:

  ◊ City library

  ◊ City hall

  ◊ Utility agency

  ◊ State highway department

  ◊ Local engineers

- Information on easements, rights-of-way, and subdivision restrictions usually come from your title company.

As you study the schematic planning, be sure that at every step the plan meets your financial objectives as well as your statement of who you are as a developer. Never lose sight of those two objectives.

Steps for Acquiring Land

DETERMINE:

- Is there a market for your project?

- What price can you pay?

- Is this price reasonable for comparable properties in the same area?

BEGIN NEGOTIATIONS

- Negotiate a price with the seller

- Ask for at least 60 days for due diligence

- Deposit Earnest money

Request steps from the seller that provide you with due diligence information, such as soils tests, hazardous waste certifications, any design or engineering studies, and governmental permits or approvals.

BEGIN YOUR DUE DILIGENCE PROCESS

Closing will typically occur about 60 days after the due diligence process is completed. You or the seller may negotiate for a longer time if it is needed. Closing can be dependent on a variety of factors, like approvals, the seller's removal of toxic waste, or other obstacles to your project.

Residential Development

REVITALIZATION

If you are interested in developing residential property, you may be thinking of new construction from the ground up, or you may want to revitalize existing properties. We call properties that are undervalued because of cosmetic or location details "artificially depressed." If you are a person who is willing to take on the risk and complexity of this kind of development, you can create huge financial rewards.

Many owners, buyers, and tenants are not able to visualize upgrades. That is why it is up to you to have the vision to see potential in an unattractive property. Many of the improvements that increase rent or sale prices are strictly cosmetic in nature. If you can estimate what it would cost you to add value, you may have a salable product with a minimal amount of effort and expense.

Public Private Partnerships

Often there are whole areas of cities that are either under-utilized or distressed. In this case, a public-private partnership between a redevelopment agency and a private developer, as well as private lenders, architects, public officials, and the community can create a high-profile, high responsibility position within the project. Redevelopment works to bring properties and new development to the community to realize their highest potential and best use. It can stimulate private reinvestment in an area, removing blight and creating business opportunities that will spur new jobs, growth and affordable housing.

Redevelopment can act as a catalyst for the entire city to begin revitalization for prosperity and balance. Increased property taxes generated from the revamped properties serve as the base for the actual funding of the project.

As a developer, you will find that the regulatory environment will be more accepting of your efforts if you team with a redevelopment agency or government entity. The public, too, will be more accepting because they will think that they have some control over the project. Redevelopment not only makes the community more attractive to visitors, but enhances economic viability and improves the safety of the region as well as the quality of life and standard of living of the residents.

Multifamily Housing

If you are considering multifamily residential development, you are most likely considering maintaining the property for rental income. Construction of multifamily housing, as with most other forms of real estate, goes in cycles. If interest rates are low, there is multifamily construction going on, offering you a good entry point as an entrepreneur.

Do you choose a site that is waiting for a building, or do you target a site depending on the market you want to reach? Experienced developers say that one must first use market information to determine what to build, and then analyze the market carefully to find niches in the market to fill. As you narrow the definition of your buyers or tenants, you will discover the site requirements that are particular to their needs.

When choosing a site, you will need to consider how compatible your project is with the surrounding land. Do you want to build apartment projects in an area that already has some successful ones? Will your high-end multifamily site fill a need for commuters who will enjoy the proximity to commercial centers? If you are planning to build upscale homes, will they match the surrounding single family neighborhood? These are all things to consider before you purchase the site.

Residential buildings may be one of several types. To decide which type of product you intend to build, you will need to consider the style, ownership, design and type of construction. Many of these decisions will be dictated by the demographics of the market, including income, age, and type of families that you choose to represent.

RENTAL APARTMENTS MAY INCLUDE ANY OF THE FOLLOWING:

- **Garden apartments** – usually two or three story housing; low density, lots of open space around the buildings, and on-site parking.

- **Low-rise apartments** – usually located in outlying areas, low rise buildings have fewer than four stories.

- **Mid-rise apartments** – can be three to 10 stories in height.

- **High-rise apartments** – also called a skyscraper, a high rise building is usually more than 10 stories high.

Owned properties can vary in their ownership arrangement and design. You may build:

- **Condominiums**, in which the purchaser acquires an individual unit plus an ownership in the common property.

- **Co-operatives**, which forms a corporation comprised of the owners. The corporation holds title to the building, and residents lease the unit from the corporation. Co-ops are not being built any more.

- **Timeshares**, in which a person retains fee simple ownership in the real estate for a specific time of the year. This is unrestricted ownership for the duration of the allotted time. Timeshares are commonly located at vacation destinations.

All of these properties can enjoy various designs that appeal to renters or homeowners from many walks of life. Clustering homes in patterns, building them back-to-back or facing each other, creating communal garage areas, and building mid-to high-rise structures can all increase the density for your location.

Townhouses can include single-level units or two- or three-level units. Many townhouse units include garages located underneath the homes, giving the area a more attractive look and freeing up outdoor space that traditionally would have been used for parking.

Four- and six-unit buildings often look like one single family home, but they are several garden apartments connected together. Attached garages and attractive landscaping help to create both beauty and privacy.

The best size for your site depends on much more than the density. You will need to consider the rate at which you can lease out the properties and see how that fits within your budget. Is there going to be an on-site property manager and maintenance staff? If so, it is important to build a site that is large enough to support this expense.

As a beginner, you probably should try (for now) to find one individual tract of land that is big enough for your building plan. Although it is done often, piecing together several tracts is complicated. If you are not able to get all the closings, legal costs, and financial backing taken care of, you may incur penalties; plus, you will have paid money for a project that now does not have adequate space to support it.

It is extremely important that you remain flexible as you target your market. Plan on basic features in your design for it to appeal to several target groups. That way, if your project is not exactly what you envisioned, it will still have appeal.

When you have a site in mind, you will study other projects around you. Specifically, you want to know:

- Rent levels

- Unit sizes

- Number of bedrooms in each unit

- Types of renters

- Average number of vacancies

Armed with this information, you have to choose whether you want to compete with the existing projects, or fill a niche that has not been met. Doing what has already been done is a "safe" way to create rental products that may have a good history. Exploring the market to find a new niche can be very rewarding as well. Ideally, your research will tell you what your market segment is and that will tell you what their price range will be. Are your potential tenants young families? Retirees? Middle-aged, affluent couples?

According to professionals in the field, there are a number of mistakes that first-time condo developers make that can be avoided. Some of these are:

- Putting family units on a third floor

- Building huge common areas that require heating, cooling and cleaning

- Pricing yourself out of your target market

- Building units that cannot be sold, so they have to be rented because you do not have cash reserves to allow you to keep them

- Reducing your own rents through design flaws (not hiding trash receptacles or carports from public view; buildings that look industrial rather than home-like)

Although your market study will start out in an informal way, somewhere along the path you probably will hire a research firm to create one for you. Lenders and investors prefer to see professional market studies, as opposed to one that you have put together yourself that could be slanted to benefit your financial backing.

Items to include in your market study:

- Assessment of capture rates each month

- Demographic analysis: Population, broken down by age groups, household size and type, total households

- Economic Analysis: employment figures, broken down by category

- Site amenities
    - Uses
    - Nuisances
    - Supply and demand figures for the area
    - Development size (square feet, stories)
    - Number of units by type
    - Construction type
    - Age of development, if applicable
    - Rent or sale price
    - Vacancies (by unit type)
    - Parking
    - Storage

- Laundry
- Elevators
- Handicapped Facilities
- Green Space
- Recreational areas
- Recreational equipment
- Unit amenities:
    - Appliances
    - Utilities
    - Cable TV
    - Window Treatments
    - Fireplaces

- Public transportation
- Private transportation
- Fire and Police districts
- Accessibility to:
    - Downtown
    - Medical centers/health care
    - Freeways
    - Schools
    - Parks
    - Day care
    - Shopping
    - Personal services

Financing Your Multifamily Project

How are you going to find a lender for your first multifamily project? You have no track record; you may or may not have the financial credit that experienced developers have. The only other criterion you have to lean on is the project itself. Its design and economic appeal must be so incredible that a lender sits up and takes notice.

If you began your career as a home builder, you may already have a relationship with a lender. That lender will already have an idea about how you treat your business, so they may be satisfied that you are able to handle the projects you propose. If you are fresh to the business, you may want to consider a small, local bank, who will keep the loan product close at hand.

Financing for income-producing properties falls under one of three types: construction loans, permanent loans, and borrowing against equity. By contrast, a project that will involve units for sale (condominiums) will only involve equity and a construction loan; buyers obtain their own permanent loans.

Equity investment is the money that makes up the difference between construction and/or permanent loans and the total project. It will generally cover about 25 percent of your total costs. Equity investors take on the greatest risk, so they usually will charge you a much higher rate to back your project. Equity investors do not receive money until after the other lenders have been paid. With an income-producing property, if the cash flow falls short, additional equity has to be pumped into the project so that the permanent mortgage is always paid.

Lenders use both your debt coverage ratio and your loan to value ratio to determine how much money they will lend you as a permanent mortgage for your project. It is calculated like this:

Debt Coverage Ratio (DCR) = NOI/debt service [NOI = Net Operating Income]

If the DCR = 1.2 or more, the lender can probably loan you the money without too much risk of default. You can calculate this yourself, but you will need to know the DCR, interest rate, and an assumed length of amortization for the loan.

NOI/DCR = monthly payments

So, if your monthly payment is $98,926, and you have a 6

percent interest rate amortized over 30 years, you would have a maximum loan amount allowed by the lender of $16,500,000.

Loan amount	$16,500,000.00
Term	30 years
Interest rate	6 %
Monthly payment	$98,925.84

The Loan to Value ratio is determined by the project's value. The capitalization rate, which is determined by the market, is applied to the NOI. The lender will usually ask for an appraisal to verify both your property's income and the capitalization rate that is applied.

NOI/CAP RATE = VALUE

VALUE X LTV = Max Loan Amount

In the example on the previous page with a monthly payment of $98,926, the NOI is $123,658. Let us use a LTV of 0.7. Therefore,

123,658 /.9 X 0.7 =$96,178

Lenders typically evaluate a property when it has reached stabilized occupancy (possibly as much as 90 to 95 percent capacity) before they fund the permanent mortgage. This mortgage may be funded in stages, or it may be a lump sum payment.

As a beginner, making optimistic assumptions about your project can result in an unrealistic financial analysis. Things you may underestimate include costs, operating expenses, and the true cost of tenant turnover. This is especially true early in the game when the costs you have on paper are an incredibly rough estimate of what you are eventually going to have. Do not make the mistake of wasting too much time trying to determine monthly costs before you have all the information about your operation and the costs of development. When you have all the information, double-check all the assumptions that you have listed so far. Analyze them. Do they make sense? Are they still accurate? As you recalculate your costs, you will get closer to the true value with each repetition.

Your market study will give you an indication of the size and type of units that you should build. The trend in recent years, even for apartment buildings, is a higher demand for luxury studio units. Other recent trends include increased security by minimizing access into the complex, exterior lighting, and good visibility to breezeways, walkways and doorways. Electronic and gated security are becoming more popular as are fences, screens, or landscaping between units.

Nationally, unit sizes are increasing. In 1990, the majority of multi-family units being constructed was between 800 and 999 square feet in size; in 2015, the majority of units were over 1,100 square feet.[iv] The demand for three-bedroom has also risen. The increase may be the result of increased use of home computers, which more affluent apartment dwellers will use in the "office" — the third bedroom. The most popular unit, though, continues to be a two-bedroom, two-bath model.

If you are building the project to sell it, you will first lease the units and stabilize the income. Buyers are interested in having as few vacancies as possible, so it is important at this stage to select reliable, permanent tenants who keep the cash flow going, even though it is very tempting to let just anyone move in. This is not the time to rent indiscriminately (like offering $99 specials) to fill up the vacancies.

You may find the terms site coverage ratio and floor area ratio when you are studying the multifamily housing market. The site coverage ratio refers to the percentage of a site that can be covered with buildings, sidewalks and parking lots. In many suburban areas, this may be subject to a 50 percent restriction (in other words, no more than 50 percent can be covered). The remainder must be green space. The floor area ratio is simply the ratio of the building square footage to the site square footage.

It will be necessary to compute operating expenses to figure your cost structure, so even if you are planning to sell your project, you will have to create some sort of breakdown of operations costs. These will include:

- **Utilities.** Common area lights, hallway lights, water, sewer and trash collection (if not included in the rental price). After the energy crisis of the 1970s, most electric and gas bills went to the renters, although some communities still pay those utility bills. There are also cable, Internet, and phone service, which you may or may not cover.

- **Maintenance.** The owner of the building maintains the exterior, capital improvements like the roof, and often cleaning for the parking lots, common areas, and lawn care/landscaping maintenance. If your project is a rental apartment building, you must also take care of all the interior maintenance.

- **Management.** These are the costs of showing and leasing apartments and collecting rental payments. The management expense may include office overhead if you maintain an on-site office.

- **Taxes.** These may be income tax, real estate tax, and licenses and fees.

Affordable Housing

In general, affordable housing is intended for either low-income renters or purchasers, particularly first-time buyers. It is made affordable through subsidized ownership or payments.

Affordability means the household pays no more than 30 percent of their income toward housing. For lower income families, the majority of their income goes toward housing costs. Limiting their costs to 30 percent or less means they will be more likely to afford other necessities that people of higher financial means take for granted.

Since the early 1990s there has been a shift that actually increased the need for affordable housing. According to the U.S. Department of Housing and Urban Development, "An estimated 12 million renter and homeowner households now pay more than 50 percent of their annual income for housing....The lack of affordable housing is a significant hardship for low-income households." This means that they sacrifice nutrition, healthcare, and savings for their families' futures.[v]

During the same time that households have become more needy, the supply of assisted housing units available has decreased because of the loss of units built in the 1960s and 70s whose contracts with private owners expired.

To add to the problem, our population is growing. A study by the Urban Land Institute reports that our population will add 38 million new residents by the year 2030 (see **www.ULI.org**). The two-parent, two-child household has given way to single parents, single households, and empty nesters who choose higher-density neighborhoods. A significant number of those will be eligible for affordable housing.

Why does this matter to you as a developer? First, you have to decide whether affordable housing is a project you would like to pursue. From a moral standpoint, many developers feel that constructing affordable homes is a way of giving to the community. By creating a project that is both profitable and well-designed, everybody wins: low-income families have more options, neighborhoods get attractive additions to their community, and developers and investors earn a profit.

The other side of developing affordable housing is that you can acquire grants, below-market financing, and direct subsidies that help offset the costs of your project. You will also have access to low-income tax credits and municipal tax-exempt bonds. Some corporations also make contributions to developers that specialize in affordable housing.

Affordable housing developers create and redevelop real estate, the same as other developers. The market may be different, but there is a clear need for it. One big difference is the financing; typically, a project may require from four up to 10 separate sources of financing.

Since federal dollars are shrinking yearly, many developers choose to seek out private and not-for-profit sources of funds.

Sources for Information and financing of affordable properties

Association of Local Housing Finance Agencies
2025 M St NW
Washington DC 20036
202-367-1197
www.nalhfa.org

Center on Budget and Policy Priorities
820 First Street NE Suite 510
Washington, DC 20002
202-408-1080
www.cbpp.org

Council of Large Public Housing Agencies
455 Massachussetts Ave, NW, Suite 425
Washington DC 20001
(202)-638-1300
www.clpha.org

Fannie Mae
3900 Wisconsin Ave, NW
Washington DC 20016-2892
(202)-752-7000
www.fanniemae.com

Freddie Mac
8200 Jones Branch Drive
McLean, VA 22102-3110

1-800-424-5401
www.freddiemac.com

Mortgage Bankers Association
1919 M Street NW.
Washington, DC 20036
(202)-557-2700
www.mba.org

U.S. Department of Housing and Urban Development
451 7th Street S.W.
Washington, DC 20410
Telephone: (202) 708-1112
http://portal.hud.gov/hudportal/HUD

Commercial Development

One of the most important points about commercial development is that the process is long from start to finish. For example, an attorney shared that his client in California had been in the process of developing a large piece of property for six or seven years before they even broke ground!

"Admittedly, it is a large property," he said. There are about 2,100 dwelling units and seven million square feet of office space; so we anticipated having issues because there were many variables. The lengthiest process was a two-year wait to select the client to develop the property."

Commercial real estate development involves raising the capital and developing commercially-zoned property for a variety of business needs. Property development may include the demolition, renovation and/or expansion of existing buildings, as well as the construction of new buildings. The commercial space may be owned, sold, or leased out by the developer.

Commercial space may include apartment buildings, retail shopping centers, strip malls, office buildings, hotels, resorts, business and industrial parks, entertainment centers and many other kinds of businesses.

A small commercial real estate portfolio probably consists of office buildings, retail developments and residential properties. At the next level it can include those as well as mid-sized industrial, medical and educational facilities. Larger companies may hold a vast number of commercial properties amassed through mergers and acquisitions and many multi-use packages.

Office Buildings

Have you considered office development for your first endeavor? Offices seem as though they would be simple and straightforward to construct; you generally have fewer tenants to worry about than, for example, a multifamily apartment complex. The nature of an office development seems to show that it is steadier than the ever-changing retail market.

What type of office building could a beginning developer consider? Generally, the scale does not matter. Whether you are looking at small or large office complexes, you will encounter the same problems and requirements. However, typically a first development will be less than 100,000 square feet or under $10 million.

Office Building Types to Consider:

- Garden Office (like garden apartments, with considerable landscaping)

- Low Rise (1, 2, or 3 stories)

- Research and Development (1 or 2 stories, containing offices, laboratory space, workshops, and storage

- Mid Rise (4-15 stories)

- High Rise (15 stories or more)

- Flex Space (1 or 2 stories, mix of offices, industrial, and warehouses)

If you are thinking of constructing office complexes, your market study should include key information about employment growth for the local economy. This is available through the Bureau of Economic Analysis (**www.bea.gov**) and will include estimates of future employment. You can use this market analysis to understand what type of tenants may come looking for a new office. Most tenants relocate their business from a fairly nearby site, rather than from out of town, so understanding the neighbors will help you understand your market.

The analysis should also help you target what types of offices will be needed. If your market contains mostly large corporate headquarters, your buildings, parking, and amenities will differ in size and structure from offices created to accommodate smaller corporations.

The purpose of the market study is to learn about employment growth and potential tenants' preferences and key requirements, such as:

- Space

- Building depth (for window offices)

- Image

- Amenities

- Identity distinction

- Regional supply (is space available? Are rents low, or high?)

- Regional conditions that may affect the market

From these items, you can project the demand. Once you have the demand in place, it is time to turn to the supply. A study of the supply is fairly straightforward and helps to identify what is available. You may also find office supply data online:

CoStar Group, Inc. **http://www.costar.com** gives data on the current market in both the United States and the United Kingdom.

After you have the supply analysis, you should be able to decide whether office space is at a deficit or a surplus for your area simply by subtracting the projected supply from the predicted demand. This should give you an idea of the vacancy rate and which direction it is moving. Compare this estimate with the concrete figures your city gives for the vacancy rate.

Although it is common to assume that your project is going to set the world on fire by outperforming all other nearby developments, you should plan to have assets available to cover a slow lease-up in case leasing takes longer than you expect.

How long should lease-up take? If the market is soft with about 24 months of existing and planned inventory, you should use that as a minimum time for your lease-up. It may well be less than that, especially if you have that truly wonderful development you predicted, but by being prepared for a lengthy wait you are covering all your bases.

Financing

Getting financing for a first-time developer who is building office complexes is difficult at best. You will have a variety of financial options at your disposal, but many of them will expect significant equity from you. Most likely, you can raise your chances of obtaining financing by preleasing your properties. Since the lease must be created so that it satisfies the requirements of the lenders, it is best to work with an attorney who is experienced in commercial real estate leases. Also, you should speak to your lenders ahead of time. Preleasing means you must have your marketing strategy in place long before the project is completed, and you will have to come up with a leasing plan showing your rental rates while the building is actually still being designed. Some developers feel that preleasing lowers their overall rental income, due to offering lower rent or making concessions, but doing so does give you an edge. You can design the space to suit the tenant's requirements. Plus, signing on larger tenants (those with prominent names, who may occupy several floors of your new building) will draw smaller tenants, and will also convince your lenders that the project is viable—and, of course, it reduces your risk.

A lender will probably expect you to put up 25 or 30 percent of the development costs in equity. Equity, as you probably recall, is the difference between the project costs and the amount you can finance. You should have your own source of equity through either your funds or the funds from your company. If not, you can establish a relationship with an outside equity investor for the duration of your project. Many developers have also begun to turn to joint ventures with lenders and tenants as a way to offset the equity requirement. Joint ventures are a great way to gain credibility with the lender, but you will give away a share of the profits and some of the control over decisions.

Items to consider when designing an office building[vi]

- Building codes

- Fire codes

- Adaptability of the design: Will it last 50 years?

- Bay depth

- Bay structure

- Vertical dimension

- Curb appeal

- Parking (allow four spaces of parking for every 1,000 square feet of interior space)

- Number of square feet per employee (average of 250)

- Exterior design

- Signage

Industrial Developments

Industrial development is the planning, design, and construction of business parks, warehouses and manufacturing sites. These projects are risky for a beginner, because it is easy to underestimate your competition. However, they give you flexibility because you can subdivide and sell the land or the completed buildings.

Business parks are popular types of industrial development. They can offer many types of space, such as:

- **Industrial parks** - containing manufacturing and warehousing facilities. These usually offer little or no office space.

- **Warehouse & Distribution parks** - containing one- or two-level storage facilities, a small amount of office space, and plenty of parking and driveway areas for truck use.

- **Research and Development parks** - offer laboratories, offices, and perhaps light manufacturing space.

- **Technology parks** - serves as a think tank for high tech companies located nearby.

- **Corporate sites** - look like office parks but the entire business goes on in the space. They often include offices, research labs, manufacturing centers, recreational facilities and conference centers.

HOW DO YOU DETERMINE INDUSTRIAL SUPPLY?

Consult market analysts and the city or county. They often offer incentives to industrial tenants to bring business into the area. Real estate brokers and management companies are an additional resource for determining who your competitors will be and how many of them exist.

Retail

If you are considering retail development, your idea may range from a single store constructed on a small parcel of land to a several-hundred-acre shopping center.

If you are building from the ground up, it is a good idea to take a middle-of-the-road approach for your first project, perhaps with a strip mall containing retail and non-retail businesses that cater to daily use. Most are considered low-density centers, with buildings only one or two stories tall and parking lots large enough to accommodate customers.

How do you determine where to locate a new retail development? As America's diversity continues to evolve, the retail shopping center changes, both in its market needs and its tenant characteristics. A shopping center will not fit into a cookie-cutter design as do some other development projects.

The International Council of Shopping Centers and Business for Social Responsibility conducted a survey in which they attempted to find reasons that retailers avoid certain areas. In this order the answers were:

1. Crime or perceived crime

2. Insufficient population in the retailer's market

3. Lack of consumer purchasing power for the retailer's product

4. Potential shrinkage

5. Rent

6. Build out/rehabilitation costs

7. Site identification

8. Inadequate parking

9. Higher operating costs

10. Construction and development costs

11. Lack of amenities to attract out-of-neighborhood employees

Types of Leases

Here is an overview of the kinds of leases you might encounter.

FULL SERVICE GROSS

A property lease in which the landlord/owner pays all the operating expenses, such as janitorial services, maintenance and repairs, utilities, and insurance.

GROSS

A property lease in which the landlord is responsible for paying all property expenses, such as taxes, insurance, utilities and repairs, but not operating expenses.

NET

A property lease in which, in addition to the rent, the tenant pays expenses, such as taxes, insurance, and maintenance, leaving the landlord with a rent receipt that is the net of those expenses, hence the name. There are various levels of net leases in which the expenses are divided between the landlord and the tenant.

DOUBLE NET

A property lease in which the tenant pays rent, taxes, insurance, and expenses that arise from the use of the property. The landlord is responsible for maintenance expenses.

TRIPLE NET

A property lease in which the tenant pays all operating expenses of the property. Operating expenses covered by the tenant can include the taxes, insurance, utilities, repairs, custodial services and license fees. The debt service and the landlord's income taxes are paid by the landlord.

TENANTS

Retail – tenant signage

Signs for shopping center tenants are an important part of your project's design. Tenants normally are expected to pay for their own signs, but you should exercise control over them through special clauses in the lease. You may want to:

- Forbid roof signs

- Forbid projecting signs

- Allow placement at a certain distance from the canopy

- Require a uniform scale, size, or placement

Signs should be related to the character you are trying to convey for your center, so that they are uniform. If your development is contemporary, you do not want Victorian-style signs, for example.

Research on environmental graphics[viii] has shown that one inch of a letter height should be required for every 30 feet of distance from the viewer to a sign. So a sign containing two-inch high letters will be visible from 60 feet away. If you are trying to attract people who are passing by in cars, you may have to adjust the size a bit because of their speed. Remember that if someone is driving, your sign has approximately five seconds to be seen and remembered. Keep text short, use clear fonts, and make sure the sign is easily understood and clearly labels the name/purpose of the business.

Good customer relations depends on:

- A strong reputation, especially for honesty and integrity

- Honoring all guarantees, warranties, or verbal promises

- Using strong lease agreements that spell out every service

- Creating a thorough list of covenants

- Creating an organization to maintain and service tenants

Clauses that allow the developer to conduct maintenance if the tenant fails to do so (at tenants' expense) will keep the property value up regardless of tenant compliance. A sample commercial lease agreement can be found on the companion CD-ROM.

Public/Private Partnerships

If you are thinking of becoming a developer, you may be tempted to skip this section. "What do I have to gain by partnering with the government?" you may ask. It can be complicated, but with the increase in urban redevelopment interests and the growing involvement of the public in municipal growth decisions, learning to partner can be profitable. The majority of major developments across the country are so complex that they could not be handled solely by a private developer nor by a government entity alone in terms of finance, design, or development. It takes teamwork and pooling of resources to create these projects successfully, as many locales have proven.

The U.S. Supreme Court gave local governments the right to create regulations for development and what is called police power (the government's obligation to protect the health, safety and general welfare of citizens) in 1915 (Hadacheck v. Sebastian) and again in 1926 (Euclid v. Ambler Realty). Since then, local governments have continued to have the right to regulate land development. Regulations seem incredibly narrow to the point of new developers' feeling as if their hands are tied.

But the use of Public/Private Partnerships (PPPs) is a centuries-old concept, and since the '70s and '80s when funding shrank, partnerships have become more advantageous for developers and the government. The partnership is an active, growing part of the real estate process.

By participating in a partnership, you may gain access to land and infill sites that you could not have reached otherwise, including many government-owned properties that may be prime pieces of real estate but that would never have been offered on the commercial market.

You will experience support throughout your development process, especially if you are backed by a "good" public partner who will encourage constituents to back the project. You will instantly earn a positive public image, as most PPPs are high-visibility projects with civic orientation.

Partnering with a government entity can provide you with a streamlined process for getting necessary approvals for the various negotiations, approvals and permits. Your design, construction and operations will be simpler with local government backing.

The public sector entities gain as well, of course; they can maximize their control over a process that they may not have otherwise been allowed to engage in legally. By offering a selective process, rather than an incentive, they can determine which private firms have access to their market. They may be able to leverage assets, although they do not own the resources to create the product themselves, and they are more easily able to create high quality goods that are beneficial to their public.

When you partner with the local government, you can often negotiate for a long-term lease on your development site, eliminating your initial investment in the land. The government entity may even share project costs with you, reducing your investment, or in the event of a shortage of cash they may be able to increase the cash flow through alternate means unavailable to private developers. PPPs also help to reduce your overall personal risk, because your partner will share in all the responsibilities of the development.

On the downside, you will have to deviate from the typical process that you use to finance, design and develop the project; working with the public causes many changes—and delays. While time is money to you, that is not the case for the public and the government, whose bureaucracies may require endless amounts of paperwork and obligations before any work can be done. A consensus must be reached before you proceed at each step, and if there is a hint of political unrest, you could be delayed even further.

In an ideal situation, the public partner will have created a clear-cut list of goals and objectives before creating the partnership. Increasingly, the developer comes to the city with an unsolicited plan for redevelopment, which the local government takes to the public for approval. The feasibility study and assessment of available resources are still the responsibility of the developer.

CREATING YOUR PARTNERSHIP

To create a successful PPP, both the local government and the development company must work together from the outset. Communication is the key to the success of the project. Some factors are going to be out of your control. For example, a typical local government may discover that it does not have the money to participate in the venture. Often such entities are not able to be involved in an active way, and a third entity, such as a redevelopment authority, must be formed to represent the public in the partnership. The objectives of the project will also be largely determined by the city.

To form a public/private venture, you will need to be sure that both parties focus on the terms of the process and collaborate throughout it by creating a business agreement early on. Be sure that the plan

1. Defines the roles of all key players

2. Defines the decision making process.

3. Defines the person responsible for each decision?

4. Outlines all milestones and deadlines.

Next, prioritize which items, resources, and expectations are to be addressed. Identify all project leaders and go-to individuals on each team. Agree on the way that interactions are to be conducted. Set up documentation procedures.

Accountability must be considered on all sides. Both teams need to outline steps for dispute resolution and create a method for assessing progress.

You can nurture the project by practicing due diligence throughout your participation in the project. You will have to abide by all requirements that are demanded: RFQ (request for qualifications), RFP (request for proposals), and all negotiations. It is sometimes easy to lose sight of the goal during the long process of development. However, if you can make it your goal to act in the best manner to create a win-win solution, you will remain ahead of the game.

KEEPING THE PUBLIC INVOLVED:

The final step in nurturing your role in the PPP is to practice strategic community outreach. There are many ways that PPPs keep the public sector in the loop. Tools that enable the public to participate in the process enhance implementation and ensure the success of the project. Some of these tools may include

- Providing fact sheets
- Websites with updates or blogs
- Open houses
- Public forums
- Surveys
- Workshops
- Polls
- Forming citizen advisory committees

WHAT TO CALL THE PRIVATE PARTNER

There are many terms used both by the government and the public partner in describing the private partner involved in a PPP. The reason is that the private sector member may be involved in design, financing, construction, operations, maintenance and management. Here we will use the descriptions set forth by the GAO[ix] to describe the many useful roles:

Building/Owning/Operating (BOO) transactions occur when a contractor builds and operates the property without transferring ownership rights to the public sector. He retains the legal title to the building, and there is no obligation on the part of the public to purchase the property or take over the title.

Build-Operate-Transfer (BOT) or **Build-Transfer-Operate (BTO)** transactions occur when the private partner constructs a specified facility according to terms laid out by the governmental agency. He operates the facility for a specific time as outlined under a contract or franchise agreement. At the end of that specific time, the private partner will sign over the rights to the facility to the governmental partner. The BTO is similar to the BOT, except that the ownership rights can be transferred as soon as the project is complete, rather than waiting for a franchise period to take place.

Buy-Build-Operate (BBO) transactions include a rehabilitation of an existing property or sometimes an expansion of an existing building. The governmental partner sells the property to the private partner, who improves the property to make it profitable.

Design-Build-Operate (DBO) transactions occur when there is an agreement between the public and private sectors for a single contract. The private partner receives a contract for the entire project including design, construction and operations of the facility. Normally, the title remains with the public sector. The DBO approach assigns the developer responsibility for the entire project to completion, and can help to speed it along if the developer is concerned that the public sector would not finish the project early enough to allow the property to be profitable.

Developer Financing transactions occur when the developer finances the construction or the expansion of a "public" building in exchange for some building rights of his own. The developer might want to build houses, commercial buildings, or industrial facilities. The facility is overseen by the government, but the developer uses his own capital and will have the right to use the facility, often even receiving income from the payment of rent payments.

Lease-Develop-Operate (LDO) or Build-Develop-Operate (BDO) transactions occur when the private partner either leases an existing facility from a public agency or buys the facility outright from the government. The private developer then invests his own capital for renovation, expansion, and/or modernization. When the project is complete, the developer may then operate it through a legal contract with the public agency.

Sale/Leaseback transactions occur when the owner of a facility, for example, a public company sells it to another entity. The property is then leased back from the new owner. This transaction could be used when the original firm does not have the capital, know-how, or other necessary resources to redevelop the property but wants to continue to use the facility in its improved form. For example, an electric company owns a building that the city wants to purchase for future use. The electric company sells the building to the city, who then leases it back to the electric company for a long term — until the city is prepared to develop or otherwise use the building. This assures the city their long-term goal while allowing the business to continue at its location.

Tax Exempt Lease transactions occur when the public partner finances the facility by borrowing the funds from a private investor or sometimes from a financial institution. The private partner gains title to the asset, but he will transfer it to the public partner at the beginning, or end, of the lease term. The portion of the lease payment that is used to pay interest on the capital investment is tax-exempt under both state and federal laws.

Turnkey transactions occur when the public agency signs a contract asking the private investor to design and build the entire facility under agreed-upon criteria. The private partner agrees to build the facility for a fixed price, will use a fast track construction method and will not have to adhere to the usual public sector procurement regulations, saving a great deal of time and some costs.

Checklist for Creating a Successful PPP

1. Define the decision-making process.

2. Make a plan of action that outlines all milestones and deadlines.

3. Set up documentation procedures.

4. Outline steps for dispute resolution.

5. Define the role of all key players.

6. Identify all project leaders and go-to individuals on each team.

7. Create a method for assessing progress.

8. Practice due diligence.

9. Practice strategic community outreach.

10. Act in the best manner to create a win-win solution in all situations.

REAL ESTATE DEVELOPMENT EDUCATION PROGRAMS WITHIN THE UNITED STATES:

Baylor University, Waco, Texas
www.baylor.edu/admissions/index.php?id=872576

University of California at Berkeley, Berkeley, California
http://groups.haas.berkeley.edu/realestate

University of Cincinnati, Cincinnati, Ohio
**https://webapps.uc.edu/DegreePrograms/Program.aspx?Progra
mQuickFactsID=2440&ProgramOutlineID=1386**

Clemson University, Clemson, South Carolina
**www.clemson.edu/graduate/academics/program-details.
html?m_id=Real-Estate-Development**

Cleveland State University, Cleveland, Ohio
www.csuohio.edu

Colorado State University, Fort Collins, Colorado
www.biz.colostate.edu

University of Colorado, Boulder, Colorado
http://leeds.colorado.edu/realestate

Columbia University, New York, New York
www.arch.columbia.edu/programs/real-estate-development

Cornell University, Ithaca, New York
www.realestate.cornell.edu

University of Denver, Denver, Colorado
www.daniels.du.edu/burns

Florida State University, Tallahassee, Florida
www.fsu.edu

University of Florida, Gainesville, Florida
http://warrington.ufl.edu/graduate/academics/msre

The George Washington University, Washington, DC
www.gwu.edu

Georgia State University, Atlanta, Georgia
www.gsu.edu

University of Georgia, Athens, Georgia
www.terry.uga.edu/realestate

Harvard University, Cambridge, Massachusetts
www.gsd.harvard.edu

Howard University. Washington, DC
www2.howard.edu

University of Illinois at Urbana-Champaign, Champaign,
Illinois
www.urban.uiuc.edu

Indiana University, Bloomington, Indiana
**http://kelley.iu.edu/Ugrad/Academics/Curriculum/page39588.
html**

The Johns Hopkins University, Baltimore, Maryland
www.jhu.edu/academics/#!/degrees=masters

Massachusetts Institute of Technology, Cambridge,
Massachusetts
http://mitcre.mit.edu

University of Michigan, Ann Arbor, Michigan
http://michiganross.umich.edu

University of Nebraska at Omaha, Omaha, Nebraska
**www.unomaha.edu/college-of-business-administration/
finance-banking-real-estate/index.php**

University of Nevada, Las Vegas, Nevada
www.unlv.edu/degree/bsba-real-estate

New York University, New York, New York
**www.scps.nyu.edu/academics/departments/schack/academic-
offerings/graduate/ms-in-real-estate-development.html**

University of North Carolina, Chapel Hill, North Carolina
www.kenan-flagler.unc.edu/real-estate

University of North Carolina, Charlotte, North Carolina
http://mba.uncc.edu/curriculum/real-estate-certificate

University of North Texas, Denton, Texas
www.cob.unt.edu/Firel

Northwestern University, Evanston, Illinois
www.kellogg.northwestern.edu/departments/real-estate.aspx

University of the Pacific, Stockton, California
www.pacific.edu/Academics/Schools-and-Colleges/Eberhardt-School-of-Business/Academics/Graduate-Programs.html

Penn State University, University Park, Pennsylvania
www.smeal.psu.edu

University of Pennsylvania Wharton Business School, Philadelphia, Pennsylvania
http://realestate.wharton.upenn.edu

University of Pennsylvania, Philadelphia, Pennsylvania
www.upenn.edu/gsfa

San Diego State University, San Diego, California
http://arweb.sdsu.edu/es/admissions/majors/realestate.htm

University of San Diego, San Diego, California
www.usdrealestate.com

St. Cloud State University, St. Cloud, Minnesota
www.stcloudstate.edu/fire/default.asp

University of St. Thomas, Minneapolis, Minnesota
www.stthomas.edu/cob

University of Southern California, Los Angeles, California
www.usc.edu/sppd/mred

University of Southern California, Los Angeles, California
www.usc.edu/lusk

Southern Methodist University, Dallas, Texas
www.smu.edu/cox

Texas A&M University, College Station, Texas
http://mays.tamu.edu/master-of-real-estate

University of Texas, Arlington, Texas
http://wweb.uta.edu/finance

University of Texas, Austin, Texas
www.mccombs.utexas.edu/Centers/REFIC

University of Texas, San Antonio, Texas
http://business.utsa.edu/refd/index.aspx

Virginia Commonwealth University, Richmond, Virginia
http://business.vcu.edu/departments-and-centers/finance-insurance-and-real-estate-fire/undergraduate-programs/kornblau-real-estate-program

State University of West Georgia, Carrollton, Georgia
www.westga.edu/mktreal

Wichita State University, Wichita, Kansas
http://realestate.wichita.edu

University of Wisconsin, Madison, Wisconsin
www.bus.wisc.edu/realestate

Nova Southeastern, Fort Lauderdale Florida
www.business.nova.edu

REAL ESTATE DEVELOPMENT EDUCATION PROGRAMS OUTSIDE THE UNITED STATES:

Hong Kong Polytechnic University, Hong Kong
www.bre.polyu.edu.hk

University of Ulster, Northern Ireland
www.ulster.ac.uk/courses/course-finder/201516/Real-Estate-5732

University of Aberdeen, Aberdeen, Scotland United Kingdom
www.abdn.ac.uk/study/courses/postgraduate/taught/real_estate2

Universidad de Alicante, San Vicente (Alicante), Spain
www.ua.es/en

University of the South Pacific, Suva, Fiji
www.usp.ac.fj

Royal Melbourne Institute of Technology, Melbourne, Australia
www.rmit.edu.au

University of Reading, United Kingdom
www.henley.ac.uk/school/real-estate-and-planning/

National University of Singapore, Singapore
www.rst.nus.edu.sg

University of New South Wales, Sydney, Australia
www.fbe.unsw.edu.au

KULAK, Belgium
www.pav.kulak.ac.be

City University London, London, England, UK
www.cass.city.ac.uk

Dublin Institute of Technology, Dublin, Ireland
www.dit.ie

European Business School (EBS), Germany
www.ebs-immobilienakademie.de

University of Western Ontario, Ontario, Canada
www.uwo.ca

Leveraging Your Investment

Leverage means using borrowed funds to finance a project, but you can think of it as your bargaining power. If you want to build true wealth, you must learn to leverage your properties. It is also important to see the value of investing in more expensive properties using the same money.

Suppose you have $100,000 to invest, and you use it to purchase an income-producing property. The return on investment in your area has been running around 8 percent. Therefore, at the end of the first year if you have not improved on your property at all, it is worth $108,000. At the end of the second year, it is worth $116,640.

Now, let us suppose you take the same $100,000, but instead

of buying a small property you use it as a down payment on a $500,000 property. You wisely select an income producing property in a neighborhood with a strong track record of appreciation in value. At the end of year one, your property is worth $540,000; at the end of year two, it is worth $583,200. You have increased your total income in only two years by $83,200— using the same money that would have made you $16,640.

Leverage is especially useful if your strategy is to purchase raw land and wait for growth to move toward it. What can you do with the property while you wait? What if it is already set up for a mobile home with a well and septic system? Could you find a mobile home for $10,000 and move it onto the property as a rental? Could you put several mobile homes there? Remember that as soon as the land becomes a viable mobile home park, its value goes up and you are able to borrow more money against the land, freeing up your investment for a different project while you are waiting for the market to change.

If you already own a small income-producing property, you might use your equity in it to finance the next property. Perhaps you are looking at purchasing land to build office buildings, and you already own an office complex that you use as a rental property. You can finance the land against the property you already own. Many developers begin this way, borrowing against each to pay for the next in a domino effect. It is a fast way to expand leverage without taking money out of pocket.

Creativity is the key to making terrific financial decisions and building wealth in your business. If a developer can look at a property and instantly see a way to make money with it, there will be numerous opportunities for expanding purchase power.

Another advantage of leverage is the tax deferment, which increases your leverage. Suppose an investor buys a home with 20 percent down and encounters a going rate of appreciation of 10 percent, converting to a 50 percent profit. For simplicity, we will neglect the costs of buying and selling. If she sells the property for a gain of $400,000, she must pay taxes of $160,000 leaving only $240,000 to reinvest. Now, suppose that instead she takes the $400,000 proceeds and reinvests with no capital gains tax. She will have the entire $400,000 to reinvest. If we assume that $400,000 becomes the 20 percent down for the next purchase, the one transaction has yielded a purchase of a $2 million property.

Leverage can greatly magnify your profit; but it also can increase your losses. This loss will feel like acceleration if the negative cash flow on the property lasts for a long time. In other words, say you have a $3 million loan on a property that is only worth $2 million. Every month, you are paying a great deal more out that the property is bringing in—especially if you are still in the construction phase—yet there seems to be no end in sight. Costs can become unmanageable, and properties are not always easy to unload if you need money quickly.

Making the decision to leverage is always a good idea if:

- The property is a sound investment (its value is likely to increase in the future).

- Your cash return is greater than your debt.

- The property has a cash flow that is continual and covers your expenses.

- You can make the mortgage payment, either from the property's cash flow or from your own income.

6

The Development Process

Finding Your First Location

Do you locate the site first and then select the market, or do you target a market and then find a site?

Most people will tell you that you should select your target market first. The site is there, you just have to seek it out. Then you can study the geographic area and the type of product and watch the real estate market cycle so that you can time your project to launch early in the positive part of the cycle.

Characteristics of the Real Estate Cycle

Try answering this question: "What is the highest and best use of the land?" You might think the answer is that the best use is tied to the highest return, without studying the demand. If you do this, you are likely to lose the highest return because demand drives the market. If the demand is not sufficient, your site will not give you a good financial return—no matter how terrific you think the idea is.

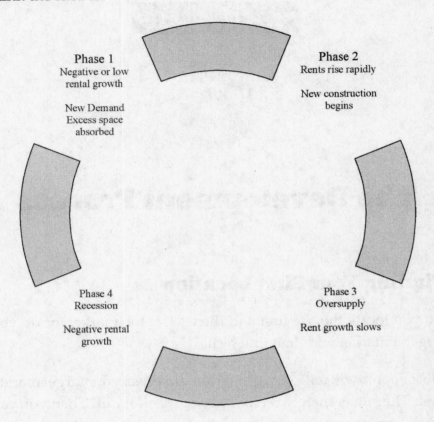

Phase 1
Negative or low
rental growth

New Demand
Excess space
absorbed

Phase 2
Rents rise rapidly

New construction
begins

Phase 4
Recession

Negative rental
growth

Phase 3
Oversupply

Rent growth slows

Site selection is probably the most important decision you will make. It is nearly impossible to straighten out a poor choice, and if you make a mediocre choice you will only get a mediocre return on your investment. Your goal, then, is to deliver the highest-quality product that will serve the needs of your local market.

Are there risks during the initial phase? Yes! You may encounter:

- **Acquisition risks**: title, easement, or other problems during your attempt to close on the property

- **Entitlement risks:** anything pertaining to getting public approval and legal development rights.

- **Site risks** may be existing physical conditions like hydrology, geology, contamination, or even botanical issues; or they may be logistical in nature like the capacity of the roads or sewer system.

- **Financial risks:** The cost of obtaining debt, equity financing, and interest rates on construction loans.

So, how do you find the right site? One strategy is to stay close to home. This will give you an advantage over national developers in terms of knowing the market. Local conditions are so much more important than national indicators, in terms of predicting the economic cycle.

Speaking of the cycle, you will find that there is a two- or three-year window in which your project is more suitable because of financing and strong market demand. After that, your chances for success decrease, and you will have less opportunity to arrange financing.

Gathering Data

You will need to validate your project to justify it for your lenders so that they will back the development. To show them there is a need for your project, you must first determine the relationship between supply and demand. Your ability or the ability of your analyst to answer these questions will give you a snapshot of market conditions and the existence of a market niche for your development.

So, what are you trying to find when you look for "need"? The demand for any type of real estate depends on the availability of jobs, and therefore income, as well as the type of households that exist in the area. For example, building an office complex out in the center of large tracts of farmland is probably not a good idea, unless you have insider information indicating that a large development company has purchased 10 adjacent tracts for exactly the same purpose. Otherwise, you will want to create a similar development to others that already have been built in the area.

To find the demand that exists for your project, you will have to understand the market. The residential market might be hot, while the demand for office and industrial space has cooled. The economy on one side of the city may be enjoying an upswing, while other parts are simply holding. Historical data is important, too. By looking at the changes that have already taken place, you can recognize patterns and see how population, income, or employment has changed over time.

So where do you begin your study? First, you want to know what the people who live in this particular area are like. You probably already have some idea if you live there, but now it is time to put what you know into concrete terms and fine-tune it.

When you are thinking about the residents in the area you have targeted — say within a five-mile radius — where do they go to eat, work, and play? Where do they shop? What is the structure of their family make-up? Do the married couples both tend to work outside the home? What kind of wages do they earn?

These are all facts that are studied by various businesses called forecasting companies. They are also often covered by the Bureau of Labor Statistics or the U.S. Census Bureau. You can gain access to these two for free, or you can pay a forecasting company for its reports.

Determine the most accurate market statistics yourself, creating estimates based on your own data. Relying on input from the experts is fine as a jumping-off point, but by having your own expert, or being your own expert, you will tailor the results to your niche. Data that has already been compiled may be outdated, tailored to the specific goals of the study, or biased. Creating your own studies allows you to consider exigent circumstances, peculiarities in the market, and the time involved. Most importantly, the data will be specific to the question you are trying to answer if you generate it yourself. Being aware of the factors involved in determining market demand will also allow you to recognize important situations that may arise and create the need for a new study to reflect changes in the demand conditions.

The demand for each type of space depends on local economic growth and other forces that can make the space attractive or unattractive to potential buyers or tenants. By studying forecasts for their underlying assumptions and by studying patterns and trends of the market, you will be able to forecast the demand for your specific development.

There are several sources of economic, financial, and industry forecasts, such as:

- Moody's Analytics **www.economy.com**

- Global Insight **www.globalinsight.com**

- Bureau of Labor Statistics (BLS) **www.bls.gov**

- Bureau of Economic Analysis (BEA) **www.bea.gov**

Metropolitan economies continually change, and the combination of factors that generates the change will help you determine the economic viability for your space. Questions like the absorption rate, the growth in rent, as well as other factors that drive the demand for your development help you learn whether your proposal makes sense.

To begin your development, you will have capital, land, market knowledge, or tenants. If you own family land, you already have the site, and your task is to search for the use for the site. If you know tenants who are looking for space, you have the use and you will search for an appropriate site.

If you do not have the land yet, but you have capital or tenants, you may try to locate a partner. Find a landowner to work with you in a joint venture; he contributes the land, and you run the development. Regardless of which field is your strong suit, you will build your partnership by finding the supporting documents to show that you can acquire the other factors needed for a successful project. For example, if you have prospective tenants, ask them to supply you with letters that you can show the lenders, or if you have market research that supports your idea, show them that.

Commercial Loan Structure

As a beginner, you may find that obtaining financing is intimidating. It does not have to be! The terms of your loan will vary from one project to another, as well as from one lender to another. Some key points to keep in mind are:

- Development loans should be structured like a revolving

line of credit, allowing you to borrow any amount up to your credit line.

- The loan could also be structured as a two-year construction loan, with up to three automatic renewals.

- Make sure the loan is large enough to cover a five-year project (or whatever term you think will reasonably be expected). Loans cannot be renegotiated.

- Points are calculated on the total loan that you request, not on your draw. That means if you are asking for a $2 million loan, if the bank requires two points to be paid up front, you will owe $40,000 in points (and usually one point per year, starting in the 3rd year).

Commercial Trends

Once you have a site in mind, you must look over the trends in your area. To study trends, you need a historical view of at least the past 10 years, as well as current data. Can you see your town graying? Is there an influx of immigrants? Has technology changed your industrial environment?

These changes may seem to be removed from your real estate development, but these changes drive the developing process. Changes in lifestyles, communication, and household makeup will create demands for an entirely different type of environment.

Some demographers have suggested that our melting pot regions will become younger, more multi-ethnic and culturally diverse. The cultural lifestyle of the areas they choose to cluster in will change, consequently changing the demand for housing that suits their identities.

Trends are shifting in retail development as well. Whereas once it was a given that the anchor store of a shopping center would be a large department store, you may find that the anchor is now a discount store, bookstore, entertainment center or even a motorcycle shop. With national chains disappearing and many regional stores reorganizing, the newer stores can take over traditional anchor spaces with nontraditional offerings. In fact, there is a term for it: de-malling.

If you are interested in redeveloping vacant mall sites, the sheer size of these anchor store slots can be daunting. They are usually 100,000 to 200,000 square feet, but can be much larger. They are subdivided into two, three, or even 40 smaller stores, which makes plumbing, heating and cooling the biggest issues. Exits, loading docks, landscaping and exterior redesign are all part of the package.

Mall redevelopment is said to address the lifestyle-centered trend of the new century. Developers are finding that they can create streetscapes, pedestrian-friendly walkways, and add in secondary stores and nighttime entertainment to enhance the big box retail and department store anchors of the new wave of shopping centers that are increasingly replacing traditional malls. They also are working more often in an alliance with housing developers to create a mixed-use niche area where residents can live, work, shop and play.

In fact, more and more retail centers are incorporating details you might find in a friendly historical Main Street setting: traditionally styled retail centers that are smaller in scope, amphitheaters, water features, architectural detailing and whimsical public art displays. The idea is that the smaller, friendlier center will evoke a soothing, safer image to draw the public in and keep them returning in a way that the traditional malls have not.

CHAPTER

7

Operations

Organizational Structure

There are many ways that a developer can choose to set up his or her company. State laws vary, but some states adapt uniform statutes to encourage commercial undertakings to be similar. Generally, you can structure a business any way you want in a formal, written agreement, but if you fail to create contracts and file them, legally your business will default to the existing statutes. Following is a sample of company organizational structures that encompass most real estate development firms in the United States today.

SOLE PROPRIETORSHIP

This is the simplest type of business you can form. You simply begin operating your business. You do not need any special documentation, unless your local government requires licenses and/or fees. You do not have to file any papers with the state. As a contractor or builder most jurisdictions do require that you have a license, as well as certain minimum amounts of insurance, but as a developer you are not required to have any special license.

On the down side, a sole proprietorship business gives you unlimited personal liability. If things go bad, you can lose your original investment and all your assets: cash, savings, vehicles, homes, and anything else of value.

You may think that this will not happen to you as long as you are careful about accruing debts during your operations, but it can also come as a result of liens or judgments that arise from personal injuries or other types of litigation. For example, an employee driving on company business could be injured in a car crash, a client could slip and fall, or you could be sued for negligence or insufficient performance. The list goes on and on, and you are responsible even if you are not aware of the laws.

Of course an insurance policy can give you some protection, but there are limits to most policy coverages. You can also file for bankruptcy to protect some of your assets, but you could also consider a different sort of business structure.

You should consult with an attorney to learn about creating and protecting a business name. You also need to have a consultation up front with an accountant who can help you consider your insurance needs, give income tax advice, and estimate your tax payments. Also, if you are hiring employees right away, an accountant can help you learn about all the various responsibilities of being an employer in your state.

PARTNERSHIP

Many businesses are set up as partnerships, either in writing or by holding yourself out as partner. We will call this a general partnership to distinguish it from a limited partnership. Often partnerships are formed because the two people have differing talents or resources to contribute to the company. One may have capital, for example, while the other has the talent to operate the business.

A partnership can consist of any number of parties. Some partnerships are formed by businesses rather than by individuals. Usually all partners are expected to do a share of the job, but sometimes they take no part in the day-to-day operations and are silent partners. Many real estate developers begin their career in a partnership. It is common to partner with a landowner to hold onto the land long enough to get it through the rezoning process, or to offer a partnership to a key tenant to entice them into leasing space in the building.

Like a sole proprietorship, in a general partnership the liability is unlimited. Any partner in the business can be held liable for the debt of the entire operation. Furthermore, if you have held yourself out as partner (meaning that the world assumes that you are partners) you may even be held liable for the acts of your partner in conducting the business. So if there is a four-person partnership in which one partner takes out a construction loan, then he and two others disappear, the remaining partner will be considered liable for the entire loan.

Partnerships that are not formalized in writing automatically are considered equal partnerships, and profits and losses will be split equally among the members. However, you can divide the business many ways. You can split the capital assets, operating income, salaries, and even levels of sales. Therefore, if you split the first $1.5 million 50-50, you may divide the next 60-40, and the next 80-20. Partners can agree on any split they like.

Partnership agreements technically are dissolved every time a partner moves in or out of the group. Written agreements can help clear up procedures that need to be followed and the obligation of the partners. Voting partners will formalize the association and the requirement to do so can keep someone from selling out their part of the business without the other members' approval. The regulations regarding the entry and exit of partners should be committed to paper. Having a legally binding contract can prevent one partner from opting out of the group. Partnerships have restructured into corporations to protect the partners' personal assets and also to raise capital through shares.

LIMITED PARTNERSHIP

Limited partnerships are like general partnerships, except for the liability aspect. Limited partnerships may have both limited and general partners. Usually the general partner(s) make policies, manage the firm, and have unlimited liability. The limited partners are investors who contribute finances and have limited liability. The limited partner is only responsible for paying out his or her investment and any profits made from the business. If you choose to have a limited partnership, you must:

- Declare it in writing

- File it with your state's secretary of state

- Pay a tax based on your income from the business

- Most likely pay an additional annual renewal fee

Limited partners are fairly silent. That is, they do not participate in the day-to-day operations of the business, nor do they create policies or make major decisions for the business. The general partners make these decisions. Hiring decisions are also made by the general partners. Thus, there must be at least one general partner in the business. The limited partners must make sure that they trust the general partner implicitly, as their investments are in the hands of this partner. If a limited partner involves himself or herself in the business's daily operations, he or she can be legally construed as an unlimited partner.

LIMITED LIABILITY PARTNERSHIP (LLP)

A LLP is a hybrid of a limited partnership and a corporation. It is used to protect the interests of limited partners who wish to participate in the daily management of the firm. LLPs are common in professional firms consisting of lawyers, doctors and accountants. The tax liability is different than that of a corporation, and this form of business is usually the best choice for real estate developers with several managers and professional interests.

LIMITED LIABILITY LIMITED PARTNERSHIP (LLLP)

The LLLP was developed to protect the personal financial assets of the general partners. The partnership is formed the same way as an LP with the same restrictions for limited partners. The filing fees for an LLLP are higher than for an LP, but the financial protections are much greater. This form of business is fairly new, and state regulations may differ, but it is most common in the real estate business.

LIMITED LIABILITY COMPANY (LLC)

An LLC is similar to an LP, but the company is structured like a corporation. All members are protected from personal liability, unless they have personally guaranteed the company's debts. The company is created as a separate entity and is taxed as such. Some states may require the company to specify the date of dissolution for the LLC. As with the LP, articles must be filed with the state and fees must be paid. However, the financial protection of having this form of business can be worth the legal requirements.

S CORPORATIONS

Large corporations such as Pepsi are known as C Corporations. The income of C Corporations is taxed twice, once as revenue for the company, and once as individual income when dividends are paid. Subchapter S Corporations were created to protect small businesses from losing significant profits from double taxation. An S Corporation is treated like a partnership under tax law, and is taxed only once. Members of an S Corp must be U.S. citizens and only one form of stock may be issued. It is also required that the firm has officers and a board of directors.

REIT: REAL ESTATE INVESTMENT TRUST

In an REIT, non-owners invest funds in the business and receive partial equity ownership of commercial real estate. The income from the firm's holdings is taxed only once. Ninety-five percent of the firm's revenue must be dispersed annually to the shareholders in the firm. There are limits on how much property can be sold in a given year, and the income distributed must come from the ownership of the real estate. These investments have an extremely high dividend rate, and so they are very popular. However, because the REIT does not retain revenue, it does not have the necessary capital to grow unless the stock is underwritten by an investment bank.

Most REITs are equity investments, that is, revenue is generated from the ownership of property. Some are known as mortgage REITs that have mortgages on real estate. If an investment has both ownership and mortgages, it is called a hybrid REIT.

UPREIT: UMBRELLA PARTNERSHIP REAL ESTATE INVESTMENT TRUST

An UPREIT is a business entity designed to circumvent immediate taxation on income. When real estate is sold to a REIT, an individual or firm may choose to create a new partnership with the REIT as the general partner. This way, the entering partner does not pay taxes on the sale of property, and the partner receives partial ownership in the firm. The UPREIT partners receive dividends from the REIT. Partners can also choose to purchase stock from the general partner, the REIT, which is considered equal to one unit of the UPREIT. Partners of the UPREIT usually choose to keep their units until they want to exit the partnership, and they then redeem units for REIT stock and sell the stock. When the stock is sold, the income is taxed. The UPREIT structure makes selling a property to the REIT more appealing, as the owners can postpone paying taxes on the sale.

JOINT VENTURES

Joint Ventures, also known as syndicates, are formed from several different firms that combine for the duration of a particular project. The resulting business can be a partnership, a limited partnership, a limited liability company, or a corporation, with each company having a predetermined income distribution.

CONSULT AN ATTORNEY, EVEN IF IT IS JUST FOR A COUPLE HOURS.

Business Structure

Aside from determining the legal structure of a business, it is necessary to arrange the internal structure of the firm. It is important to identify everyday activities and decide who should do them and when they should be done. While small businesses have fewer employees and can be less formal than large organizations, they must still assign responsibility and authority to specific people.

Donna Jones is an attorney with Sheppard Mullin Richter & Hampton in San Diego, CA. Ms. Jones specializes in entitlements, CEQA issues and permit processing. She says that no matter what size firm you choose to operate, "get recommendations for the best consultants, build a great team, and use that team. Meet frequently and gather input from all sources."

The keys to having a successful organization are proper planning, clear relationships, and the delegation of responsibility and authority. Employees need to know or be able to find out who is in charge and who can answer their questions. They need to understand what their own responsibilities are and how they fit into the business unit as a whole.

There are several different ways to organize a business. In the very beginning, the business structure will be very loose. The developer will be driven by opportunities as they arise rather than by a business model. As a start-up entrepreneur, a developer will build to suit or build on speculation so that few employees are needed.

As the company begins to grow, most small businesses are divided into only two categories: the owners and the employees. The owners are able to make quick and effective decisions, but they are responsible for all of the operations of the business. Workers have little or no authority and report directly to the owners. As the business expands, the firm must be reorganized to reflect increased demands on the owner's time. Owners may choose to organize the business into departments based on functions. This structure allows each manager to specialize in certain tasks and to maximize efficiency in everyday operations. The problem with this structure is that managers may lose sight of how their department fits into the firm as a whole, and rivalries between departments can develop.

Some owners may choose to organize their business based on the business enterprise or product being developed, allowing managers to focus only on the steps related to their specific projects, but doing this can result in duplication of effort. For example, all managers would have to perform accounting tasks

Regardless of the specific organization, it is important that every firm have an organizational chart showing a clear chain of command. People cannot do their jobs efficiently if they are unsure of what their specific responsibilities are and to whom they should report any problems. Employees must have one supervisor only. Having more than one supervisor can force an employee to choose between two sets of instructions or to divide time to complete tasks. Having one supervisor maximizes efficiency and minimizes any communication problems.

Also ensure that managers are not in charge of too many

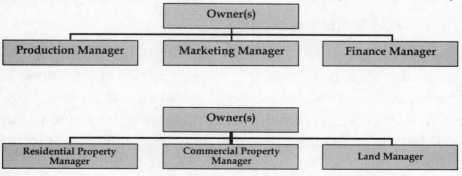

employees. Generally, each manager can have five or six employees comfortably, and a few more if the employees under the manager need little supervision or guidance. Having a low manager to employee ratio ensures that each employee's concerns or problems will be addressed by the manager and that the manager has enough time to supervise everyone.

Accurate and comprehensive job descriptions are invaluable to a firm. Putting job descriptions in writing reduces redundancy of effort and friction among employees. Have you ever had anyone tell you that it is not his or her job to correct a problem the company they work for has caused you? While this nonchalant attitude is deplorable, it is important that employees be aware of their responsibilities and their coworkers' responsibilities. Knowing who is in charge of what allows an employee to direct other workers or to go to the responsible party promoting communication and minimizing time spent gathering information. Also, if employees have a strong sense of how their job relates to the other positions within the firm, they will be able to perform their tasks more effectively and responsibly. By understanding the big picture they can clearly interpret situations and assignments and know what the overall result should be.

MANAGEMENT STRUCTURE

The next big step in structuring your business is distributing authority. Managers could never get their own jobs done if they were forced to lead their employees around all day. Thus, with responsibility comes authority or decentralization—the distribution of decision making power to different levels of the hierarchy. The decision on how much a business should be decentralized rests with the owners and general managers, and it is a hard decision.

Managers should not try to maintain control of a business by micro-managing their employees, but rather by being more careful and diligent in the hiring process. Every employee's key strengths and weaknesses should be given consideration in the initial setup. Their capability in making decisions and their integrity are very important. An employee cannot accomplish a task if he or she cannot gather the information, materials and manpower needed to see the project through.

PR and Publicity

Public relations plays a large role in the success of your company whether you are on site or off site. Developers who are active in the community with civic organizations, churches, the chamber of commerce and other groups usually create a good off site public image. When you are on site, you create a good impression through the appearance of your site and your office, the way your staff treats visitors, and the way that you present yourself.

PR professionals are good contractors to hire to maintain high profile public relations. A PR professional will know when an event is newsworthy and will publicize the event. Some examples are:

- Your purchase of the land

- Successfully closing the loan

- Breaking ground or grand opening

- First residents move into a new subdivision

- Special features of the project, especially if they can tie in with human interest stories

- Special events

- New or unusual elements of your design

PR firms can also create newsworthy measures on your behalf, by staging press parties, previews, or fund-raising events. They may create newsletters that go out on a regular basis ranging from once a year to monthly, and target those letters to go to residents, employers, brokers, prospective tenants, area stores, or community-based organizations. These letters serve to attract buyers and tenants, as well as to let the public know that you are serious about your relationship with them.

Target your message to the various audiences in the public. The following chart gives a guideline of possible messages to convey.

GROUP	MESSAGE
Landowners	You have the ability to carry through with the project.
Lenders & Investors	You are able to repay loans and deliver what you promise.
Government Entities	You take care of customers and act as a caring, responsible citizen.
Competitors	You share a mutual respect and are willing to work together in the business.
Customers	You are concerned about their wants and needs.
Potential Employees	Your company will be a positive and profitable experience for them.
Media	You are respectful of their time and willing to share your information with them.

High Profile PR

New companies have to work hard to build their name in the marketplace. In fact, many spend thousands of dollars on advice from professional consultants, who recommend that they spend thousands more dollars. But a clever business owner can carry the company a long way to get high-profile publicity with little cost involved.

Make a habit of creating press releases that are sent to every related newspaper, magazine, TV station and radio station in your area. Do this every time you have something new to announce. Highlight certain aspects of your structure, such as architectural amenities or its contribution to green building. Even if only one media center carries your story, you will gain potential access to thousands of potential clients. The best press releases use:

- A headline that grabs attention

- Very few words

- Clear, concise writing

Use the Internet. A home page is fairly inexpensive, and if it is set up correctly it will draw many visitors to the site. Be sure that your site is search engine optimized, and that it carries the name, address, phone number and email address of your business. Post your company bio and press kit where everyone can see it. Provide interesting information like photographs of your progress and update it often. There is low-cost advertising through Google, Yahoo, and other search engines that can drive plenty of customers and potential investors to your website.

Direct mail and the Yellow Pages are proven methods of

advertising that build your name. There are very few small businesses that can effectively create their own direct mailings; it is easier to find a mailing list vendor to handle your campaign. Direct mail is especially useful to announce the grand opening of your project to potential buyers or tenants.

Be a do-gooder. Sponsoring a Christmas tree sale, helping build Habitat for Humanity homes, donating to charities, and public speaking will promote your company and put your name in a positive light.

Prize drawings, like giving away a free piece of land, are an easy way to promote your new development. Some developers actually give away a house in return for an entry fee, which pays at least part of the cost of the property. The publicity from this gimmick can often bring in enough traffic to pay for itself several times over.

Trade shows are expensive, but the really good ones can build your business. At a trade show, be aware that most of the trade journals have deadlines that are several months in advance. Provide them with press releases and press kits in time to meet their deadlines. Be sure to make plenty of press kits beforehand that are lightweight and creative. Include a one-page company bio and a brochure about your latest project. After the show, be sure to follow up with everyone you met.

Model homes are an important part of selling or leasing residential properties. A model unit gives the customer a sense of how the home will look when it is lived in. Normally the units that are decorated sell very quickly; in fact, one Fishkill, NY, developer recently revealed that the expense of decorating model units ranged from $100,000 to $130,000 on homes that sold for around

$465,000 to $527,000.[x]

Model units need to be:

- Located near the sales office

- Decorated lavishly (see list below) with small furniture to make them seem larger

Model units also should use mood lighting, soft music and attractive colors. Do not be tempted to create built-ins that are not part of the standard plan as they tend to confuse customers and create problems.

MODEL HOME DECORATIONS

The current trend in decorating is to create a sense of beauty and comfort. Some suggestions include:

- Baking cookies or fresh bread in the oven (for the smell)

- Houseplants

- Decorative objects

- Fine art

- Plush area rugs

- Mirrors

- Removing doors to give a spacious feel

- Placing a wine bottle and glasses in the master bedroom or by the whirlpool tub

- Placing rose petals in the bedroom or bath

- Using upscale wall coverings

- Putting toys in the children's areas—and encouraging them to play there!

8

Management

Creating the Right Team

Your success as a developer is going to depend largely on your ability to multitask, but addressing the myriad of financial, physical and political activities that are connected to your project may be impossible without help. Even seasoned developers find it a challenge to stay abreast of every technical detail of a project. That is why they hire professionals.

Most start-up businesses have two goals in mind. One is simply to complete the project, and the other is to cover all the overhead costs. It seems that those who do better in the long run are the ones who concentrate on being able to cover all the overhead costs for the project. By doing this for your first few projects, you can ensure a small but ongoing success.

When you are considering assembling key players for your team, you can either hire staff members or consultants. Most people create some combination of the two in the beginning. You may want to hire consultants on a project basis to start.

Who should be on your team? At the very least, you will need an office manager or executive assistant who can handle calls from customers, lenders, investors and other team members. This will be the only employee in the beginning and can be hired on a consultant basis. An accountant is also an integral part of any business model, as is an attorney. Besides these key players, you will need a design and construction team, or at the very least an architect and a general contractor.

Beginning developers seem to make one of two mistakes when considering personnel for their firm. The first mistake is to overextend yourself. If you do not outsource enough of the work, you may end up not answering the buyers' or tenants' concerns quickly enough, giving the customer a bad impression.

The other beginner mistake is on the opposite end of the spectrum. Instead of not hiring enough personnel, you might hire too many. A huge staff is not required, even in a large office. Instead, concentrate on finding staff members who are:

- Extremely qualified in their area of expertise

- Self-motivated

- Aggressive

- Honest and ethical

- Personable (especially if they are working with the public)

Although larger firms usually assign team members to one function—like finance, construction, marketing, or leasing, smaller firms tend to hire team members to cover various functions. Your structure can be formalized later, but at the beginning everyone is going to report to you anyway. You will have plenty of time in the future to delegate some of your authority. You may want to hire a consultant who can help you create your business plan and structure your personnel in an effective way.

How to Pay Personnel

If you are interested in hiring a project manager, as many beginning firms do, one of your biggest decisions will be deciding how to pay him or her. Some companies believe in giving equity in the firm, especially since it is difficult for beginners to pay market rates for their services. Having a stake in the company gives the project manager a bigger incentive to work toward the future.

To attract a top-notch project manager, you may have to pay out as much as 25 percent of your profits. As you become better established and known in the field, you will pay less. Compensation packages for managers as well as other employees vary greatly from one firm to the next. Some employees are looking for good benefits, some would like a large salary with a small bonus at the end of the year, and some prefer a smaller salary but a large incentive package. The way that you compensate your employees can be developed into any number of creative packages.

CONTRACTORS

The contractors you hire for your development will be the builders and their managers who create the reality you have drawn on paper. If you have a talent in this area, you may serve as your own contractor, but many developers run their business successfully with no knowledge of the contracting business.

A general contractor (GC) is someone who contracts with developers to build projects according to their plans or specifications. If you are working with a GC, you will draw up the specs, usually with the assistance of an architect and/or an engineer, and the contract will contain terms like the price and a set deadline. The GC will divide the contract between several subcontractors to complete the assignment: excavation, concrete work, carpentry, mechanical, electrical and plumbing will all be performed by different subcontractors. The GC oversees their work performance, making sure that the quality is up to your requirements and that the work is completed within the designated time frame.

If you are interested in hiring a GC, you should contact a number of firms and ask them to submit their qualifications. They should submit descriptions of past projects, résumés of their various key employees, references from clients, details on their employees' experience, references from lenders, and verification that the company is bondable. You will then open the project for bidding, generally choosing from the top three to five contractors who turned in their qualifications.

When you are deciding between contractors, it is important that you match your project with someone who is familiar with your product. You do not want to hire a contractor who has mostly built single family homes. Look for a contractor who has more than twice your workload in total business. In other words, if your project totals $10 million, your contractor will have $30 million in total current business.

Be sure that you check the contractor's references! Talking at length with past clients will give you a clear picture of what you can expect from your contractor during the construction process.

Developers of larger scale projects might hire a construction manager, or CM, to oversee development. A CM can advise your team on ways to control costs during design. You may hire your CM only for preconstruction consulting, or you may also extend the contract into the construction process, in which case the CM handles the role described above for the GC.

Some of the activities that may be included in the scope of the contractor's job are:

- Design process

- Land planning

- Architectural design

- Electrical design

- Natural gas design

- Technology (phone, IT, cable) design

- Soil science

- Surveying

- Environmental studies, stream and wetlands delineation

- Preconstruction

- Development scheduling

- Vertical construction scheduling

- Pre-bid meetings

- Bid process

- Marketing

- Permitting

- Bid review

- Recommendation of contractors

- Site inspections

- Code compliance

- Preconstruction meeting

- Weekly construction meetings

- Testing engineering

The contractor's job is to complete the physical construction of the project on time and on or under budget. The contractor who has been selected should complete a construction cost estimate based on the drawings supplied by your architect. He or she will then set up a schedule for loan disbursement from the lender.

You will find that contractor fees are based on the size of the project, the amount of anticipated change orders, and the total costs. The largest alteration of your overall budget will come from change orders that occur when the architect's plans change because of practicalities in design, market design strategies, or unavailability of materials. Monitor all change orders to keep your costs under control.

How are contractors paid? Generally, they are paid through either bids or contracts. A lump sum bid is normally used when the design is established and total expenses are determined before hiring the contractor. About 5 percent of costs might be a reasonable starting point for calculating your contractor fee. As a new developer, it would be best to avoid paying a percentage fee as it does not give the contractor any incentive to save you money on construction costs.

To help keep costs to a minimum, you can offer an incentive to the contractor. For example, offer him or her a percentage of your savings on the total project costs (subtracted from the maximum). Payments should be offered in increments so that if the job is not completed, you have the funds to hire another contractor to complete it.

Be sure that your contract has a beginning and an end date, with incentives to finish on time or, alternatively, penalties for NOT finishing the project by the completion date. If you alter the costs or the finish date, be sure to amend the contract in writing. Obtain a detailed schedule with incremental milestones before the contractor starts work. Having the schedule on hand will allow you to track the progress of the job, anticipate any setbacks and be aware of all critical activities that can delay the project. Familiarizing yourself with the schedule will give you more control over the completion of the project.

Employee or Independent Contractor?

Sometimes it is hard to know whether you are hiring someone as an employee or an independent contractor, and sometimes you agree to use an independent contractor only to have your accountant call the person an employee for tax purposes. The difference is that as an employer you have certain responsibilities, like Medicare, social security, and worker's compensation, which you should be paying.

Additionally, you should withhold taxes from the paycheck of an employee, whereas you would never do that for an independent contractor who files his own taxes. According to the Internal Revenue Service, if you control when and how the work gets done, as well as the person's pay, you are an employer. However, if you contract with a plumber, for example, to complete a job, he or she is not necessarily your employee. In this case you are not dictating how they do the work or how many hours it will take. Instead you are agreeing that for a certain sum of money the person will complete the job. That is what independent contractors are.

You will still file reports with the IRS, particularly the Form 1099-MISC, if you pay a contract worker at least $600 for services. What you will not be responsible for is the taxes and insurance for that particular worker.

Human Resource Policies

If you are going to have employees, it is essential that you have a written employment policy to outline your basic rules as to Equal Opportunity Employment, harassment, the types of employment that you offer, confidentiality agreements and at-will terms of employment.

If you receive federal funding, you must comply with affirmative action/non-discrimination policies. In addition to learning about those laws, business owners must post these policies on the walls in a conspicuous place at the main location of the business. It is also a good idea to create an employee handbook

An employment handbook will spell out the rules, like whether Martin Luther King Day is observed, or whether the employee gets paid time off to go to the dentist. It will save you time and boost your employees' morale. With clearly stated rules, you will have a good chance of creating a positive image for your company in the community. This reputation of having a good place to work will lead to better applicants when you have job openings.

Most of all, an employee handbook or list of employment rules will help your employees know exactly what is expected of them. They will know what type of performance will give them a chance at a promotion or a raise, and they will know about your "house rules," like confidentiality.

In addition to providing your employees with a written policy, there are certain documents that you should maintain for yourself. Some that pertain to the hiring, employing and termination of employees are:

- A complete file on each employee

- Documentation of the handbook and related policies

- Performance evaluations on a regular basis of every employee

- Personnel files to back up your information, which meet employees' privacy rights

WRITING AN EMPLOYEE HANDBOOK

When developing your handbook, try not to include clutter; instead, be short and concise so that it is easy to understand. Some things you will want to cover are:

A company overview. Tell, in a few sentences, about its history, goals, ethics and your management philosophy.

Equal opportunity. Your employees' religion, age, sex, or race have nothing to do with whether you hire, promote or terminate, or how you will distribute pay or benefits.

Work hours. Define the work week, time allowed for lunch and breaks, and holiday schedule.

Compensation and performance issues. Present general statements about when paychecks will arrive, your classification of employees (part-time, full-time, on-call), and policies on pay advances, leave, overtime and other pay irregularities. Many states have laws determining how soon after your pay period you must pay your employees, as well as other laws about leave. Be sure you are in compliance with your state's laws before writing your manual.

Performance review policies. Employees should know how they will be evaluated and how often. This section should also discuss your hiring policies and how you will notify them of unsatisfactory performance.

Benefits. Health insurance and parental, or maternity leave should be discussed in detail. Who is eligible for insurance? How long after a new employee is hired will he wait for coverage? What is the company's percentage of the premium?

Insurance is usually best spelled out by providing employees with brochures from your insurance company.

Leave. Explain policies on vacation, sick leave, military leave, funeral leave, personal time, family leave, medical leave and jury duty. List all paid holidays.

Standards of conduct. One of the main reasons to create an employee handbook is to ensure that employees and staff understand what you expect of them. Discuss dress code, timeliness, policies on sexual harassment and discrimination, use of alcohol, drugs, and tobacco in the workplace, pre-employment screening and post-accident drug testing. Outline your disciplinary and grievance procedures.

Termination. List the reasons for which you will fire an employee. They might include dress code infractions, poor performance, dishonesty, insubordination, absenteeism, violations of company policy, criminal activity on the job, health and safety threats.

Property Management

As a developer, you must try to maintain positive relations with many different types of groups: the public, your investors and lenders, and the people you hire to work for you. But the most important step you can take is to ensure the satisfaction of your customers, whether they are tenants or home buyers. These are the people who will mean the most to the success of your venture.

After you have constructed and leased out your commercial or multi-family development, your focus becomes totally operational. You will expend most of your effort trying to keep your occupancy as well as your rental rates as high as possible. You may choose to hire this job out to a professional, or you may want to hire your own staff to manage the property.

Management of your property can determine whether it is a profit center or a loss. It can be very time-consuming, especially if you have a very small staff. The skills of your staff may not lend themselves to managing leased properties, but keeping management in-house allows you to

- have closer contact with tenants and the person you have chosen to maintain it.

- create an income stream.

- have better insight into the needs of the tenants to help you develop a better project the next time.

Should you hire an outside property manager? A property manager can perform many jobs to free you up to develop other properties particularly if you feel that you have no time or expertise to handle the day-to-day management aspect of the business, and a manager can save you money as well as time. The duties of a property manager might include:

- Leasing – showing property to prospective tenants as well as handling contracts and deposits from current ones

- Supervising move-in

- Collecting rent

- Paying expenses

- Maintaining common areas

- Property repairs (hiring contractors and overseeing projects)

Expenses include mortgages, taxes, insurance premiums, payroll and maintenance. If the property has a community association, the homeowners will pay their own mortgages and real estate taxes but the property manager (in this case a community association manager) must collect the association dues.

Additionally, property managers must oversee contracts for regular janitorial, grounds maintenance, security and trash removal services. They supervise these services and resolve problems with the tenants concerning the services that are supplied.

Further responsibilities of an experienced property manager will include knowing how to comply with legal issues like the Americans with Disabilities Act and the Federal Fair Housing Amendment Act. He or she must also be aware of and comply with local fair housing laws as well as the local, state, and federal building codes.

Hiring a property manager will require that you find experienced firms or personnel, usually located through the Institute of Real Estate Management. You should visit properties the firm is currently handling so that you can get a sense of the quality of their work. A good manager will be able to create a schedule of operations showing you how often they will perform inspections, maintenance and replacement. In addition, good property managers can budget for the fiscal year so that they both reduce operating costs and offset emergency repairs.

One advantage of hiring a property manager, especially if he or she is located on-site, is that any problems a tenant may have can be solved more easily. If the manager handles complaints effectively, the positive communication helps your reputation. However, if tenants are going around the property manager and bringing complaints directly to you, your manager may not be handling problems effectively. Because it is your reputation at stake, this sort of problem needs to be addressed right away.

An on-site manager will be responsible for enforcing rent collection, parking rules, restrictions on pets, and lease termination or eviction procedures. He or she may hire a leasing agent, or advertise the property for lease on your behalf, setting rental costs to be competitive in the current market.

It certainly is not necessary for small properties to have an on-site property manager; many make do without it. Some developers hire one manager for several properties. In this case the person acts as your portfolio manager.

Property managers are generally paid a percentage of the gross revenue of the property ranging from 1 percent to 5 percent, depending on your geographical location. Occasionally fees are set at a per-unit amount, but this custom is less common. If you are unsure of the fees in your area, opening the job for bidding can give you a good comparison. Study the bids carefully to see what part of the fees are included and which ones they expect to bill separately. The cost of maintenance, labor and materials for the outside vendors that the property management firm will hire are never included in the bid. They are a separate expense.

Asset Management

If you are choosing not to sell your development, the property becomes one of your assets. You will either manage the daily operations yourself or hire a property manager to do so. It is usually more costly to hire an on-site manager, so you may choose to go with a professional management company for now.

Some developers put their properties in the hands of real estate asset managers, whose job it is to act as the developer's agent and adviser for the property. An asset manager will plan not only daily operations but also long-term strategic financial plans. Asset managers direct the purchase and lease as well as the sale of real estate on your behalf.

Asset managers consider many factors when making decisions about your property, including property values, population growth, surrounding development, zoning changes, taxes and transportation issues. They consider your property's value and determine whether it is turning enough profit for your company's benefit, or whether it should be sold. The contract that you have with your manager should spell out who is performing each of many duties, including:

- Signing leases

- Authorizing expenses

- Advertising

- Banking

- Keeping records

- Insurance

- Protection or security against damage or loss

- Managing employees

Low Cost Marketing

As a developer, you want to build your brand as well as promote your project before it is even built. The Internet offers you a terrific medium for doing just that.

Promoting a residential project requires that you present to four different audiences: buyers, tenants, investors and realtors. If you have a retail development, you have the added responsibility of helping your tenants promote to their own customers. By creating a thorough Internet marketing strategy, you can address all of these groups.

You can attract leads through search engines, listings directories, display ads and affinity websites. You can also use calls to action, databases and computerized customer relations strategies. It is easy enough to add an email opt-in list, or create an in-house email list. Social media sites are also an important media tool. Most of these sites reach large audiences and can create interest in your project with little to no added cost.

Good asset management means two things: being able to protect your investment so that you can present a salable product at any point in time, and knowing how to add value to it.

When will you sell a development? Let us take an office building as an example. You have completed the project and started lease-up. Occupancy has begun to stabilize. You may choose to sell at this point, or you may choose to wait until after the first year to get the highest return on your investment.

Your third option would be to hold the property for a long-term investment (seven years or more) before selling.

Preparing for a Sale

Cash flow is your most important selling tool. It is what buyers will be looking at when making their buying decision. You can choose to increase your short term cash flow, but some steps may actually lower your long-term profit. For example, you own an apartment building and you drastically lower the rent for a month or two (with rates increasing back up to normal thereafter). Now you have a new crop of renters, but can they actually afford the higher rates, or will you create more expense and headaches trying to evict them?

Other ways to prepare for a sale might include cutting back on operating expenses or other expenditures. However, a savvy buyer will see that the reductions you have made are only temporary. He or she will factor in the difficulties of unreliable tenants or capital expenditures when planning his or her offer on your property.

Should you tell the tenants about an upcoming sale? Most experts say no. However, you should notify them in writing immediately after a sale, and in some states, the law requires you to do so within a given time.

One sales practice that many developers are beginning to use is the sale of newly built properties at auction. This is particularly effective with properties that have many units, like condominiums. Of course, some of the units sell for less than the premium price. So what is the attraction? It is the fact that, rather than holding onto the units for two, three, or even five years, the developer sells them all within a day — sometimes even within an hour! The lower sales price is offset by the fact that he or she does not have to continue to carry the property.

CHAPTER 9

Finances

Financing Your First Venture

First-time, unknown developers have few options when looking for financing. You may wish to use your own money, but it is easier to use someone else's money if you can do so without putting the fundamental details of the deal at risk.

Real estate lenders earn their money on the fees they get from loaning you money. They are not interested in obtaining equity through the success, or failure, of your deal.

Craig Evans, of CP Development, LLC, says that there are "many opportunities for oversights. You are always thinking that you should have been aware of this or that.... There is an almost unlimited scope of how many things can go wrong."

One way that Evans tries to stay prepared for mishaps is to plan his resources carefully. "Whatever you think the costs are going to be, tack more on top. You are going to get to the [financially strapped position], and if you do not have adequate resources, that is when it gets dicey."

Evans suggests trying to get loans that match the somewhat inflated numbers that will eventually be your realistic cost plan and then being aggressive in shopping for financing. "If you are brand new, definitely find a local source that wants to establish a relationship with you…but then graduate a level and shop your financing. Lenders will compete for your business. Be aggressive."

In fact, lenders do want to do business with you. It is, after all, how they earn their money. They have rules and policies, but within that framework they are more than willing to work up a loan that is tailored to your needs. And once you have created a reputation that is familiar to several lenders, you will find that you can usually negotiate for the loan terms and type of loan that you want.

One proven strategy that many developers use is to find added value opportunities, meaning that real estate does not have a concrete value. So if you can add value and get an appraiser to agree that the new value is the true value of the property, you can go back to your recalcitrant lender and ask for a bigger loan.

Evans says, "Interestingly, even though we have a good relationship with several lenders, we shop for lending on each project. We even go so far as to let them know they are competing with each other…. It is amazing how much more competitive they get. Competition becomes really important when you are trying to get a project financed."

When asked whether the pressures and risks associated with real estate development ever get him down, Evans said, "Not really. I have not had sleepless nights, but occasionally a wrinkle in the plan makes you take a deep breath and say, 'I have got to come up with a million bucks. Where do I get that?'"

Final Pro Forma

Pro forma statements are used in reports that you prepare for outside entities such as creditors, potential investors and company owners. Businesses that apply for loans to fund projects are often asked to submit a pro forma statement with the application. Your objective in providing this statement to the financial institution is to show them how the new loan would affect the current assets and liabilities of the company. They will use the comparisons of your various pro forma financial statements to predict the projection of your company's future performance. In fact, the SEC requires pro forma statements with any registration or proxy statements by companies that are listed on the stock exchanges, so they are considered part of a normal accounting practice.

If you have changed your accounting principles or the way that you estimate the value of your assets or if you have acquired or disposed of assets or changed the partnership, it may be time to recreate the financial statements. You will also need to change them if you find an error in a previous report. The pro forma statements are useful for assessing financial changes because they show you the impact of the changes on your company's financial position. You will find these effects on your income statement, balance sheet, and on the cash-flow statement. Fill out the pro forma statements to compare the consequences of refinancing your debt, joining forces with another business person, or other changes that could impact your bottom line.

BE SURE THAT YOUR FINAL PRO FORMA STATEMENTS SHOW:

- Your salary

- Salaries of your employees

- Applicable taxes, including corporate state franchise taxes

- Partners' capital in the contributed capital section

- Changes due to pooling interest if you are merging two companies

A savvy business owner uses them to construct an annual budget as well as other planning. They are also useful when choosing between capital expenditures.

Debt Service

Getting financing for your first development will be the most difficult to obtain. You will need enough equity to cover your predevelopment costs, plus some of your other costs. Equity can be obtained from private investors or lenders. For a first development, though, it usually either comes from your own pockets or the pockets of your friends and relatives!

Your interim financing (construction loan) is usually offered with a 12 to 24 month deadline. During that time, it is not amortizing. You will normally have a monthly draw that is set to cover a certain percentage of your costs.

You will find that you are required to keep the construction loan until your project has reached a stable state — if it is an office building, for example, you will wait until lease-up has started and occupancy is stabilizing. This might mean that you have reached a certain number of occupied units, usually 75 to 80 percent, or it may mean that your one-year leases have matured to a certain point.

When you are ready to exchange your construction loan for a permanent one, you can expect to finance up to 75 percent of your property's value, subject to a 1.2 to 1.3 debt service coverage ratio. You will want to check on the current cap rate.

	1ST QTR	2ND QTR	3RD QTR	4TH QTR
East	20.4	27.4	90	20.4
West	30.6	38.6	34.6	31.6
North	45.9	46.9	45	43.9

Accounting & Bookkeeping

Who is going to manage your budget? Pay the bills? Make sure that your plan stays on track with economics? Communicate with lenders and investors? This end of your business is an entire book unto itself and is usually handled by a finance manager.

As a beginner you may not have someone on hand to manage your system. If possible, you should at least have an administrative assistant—even a part-time employee—to handle your finances. If that is not possible, here are a few ideas for making the financial end more manageable.

ACCOUNTING

Day to day operations will probably take up most of your time and energy, but you must attend to the financial side of the business as well. Some sample forms are given at the end of this chapter and on the companion CD-ROM to help you get started with bookkeeping.

Accounting is the process you use to manage your cash flow. You, or someone you hire to perform your accounting will record, report and analyze all your financial data. Every business has to keep track of its money for the IRS as well as stockholders, investors, lenders and employees. Without putting thought into your system, your budget, cash flow and bills will quickly spiral out of control.

You can hire an accountant to set up and keep your books, or you can try using accounting software like QuickBooks. You will record each transaction onto a balance sheet, whether on paper or a computerized version. The sheet will contain a system of debits and credit (this is referred to as double-entry accounting), and every transaction will be recorded so that at all times your assets are equal to your liabilities plus capital.

$$\text{Assets} = \text{Liabilities} + \text{Capital}$$

You will need to use periodic reporting for your accounting system. The following is a suggestion for your system:

- **DAILY** – Record transactions, including all purchases, invoices, cash in and draws on your loan. They can be kept either in a journal or on a special page in your accounting software. Some people maintain several journals, such as one for cash receipts and one for disbursements.

- **WEEKLY** – Post your debits and credits to a general ledger that is a summary of all your business journals. The ledger should show accounts payable, accounts receivable, your equity and list your other accounts.

- **MONTHLY** – Make adjustments to the general ledger. These adjustments allow for things that occur that you may not record in your daily journals, such as accrued interest, taxes due, and bad debts. The purpose of the adjustment is to make the revenues match the expenses.

- **YEARLY** – Close the books and post your net profit into the equity account. Bring revenue and expense accounts to zero. Prepare financial statements that summarize all your financial activity for the year.

Financial statements show the financial health of your business. You and your management team will use the data to plan your company goals, make projections about revenue and expenses, keep track of your cash flow, and monitor your costs. People outside the company (present and future employees, potential investors, stockholders, lending institutions, etc.) will also want to see how you are performing financially.

If you keep your financial statements current, you will be able to prepare your tax returns more easily and make reports to the IRS. Some of the statements that are most common are:

- The **Income Statement** - An income statement is a summary report that lists various revenues and expenses from business operations during a given period— a year, a quarter, or a month. The difference between revenues and expenses represents a company's net income or net loss. Income statements are important to you as a business owner because they represent your bottom line.

- The **Statement of Capital** – This report shows changes in your capital accounts over time. The capital account represents how much of your company you own. The statement of account is prepared after the income statement, so that you know whether the company has a profit or loss. At the close of the accounting cycle, any net income becomes yours. You can choose to reinvest it in the business, pay yourself a personal income or withdraw all of it.

- **Balance Sheet** – Gives you a quick overview of your company's financial position at any point in time. As described above, the balance sheet is based on

    ◊ Assets = Liabilities + Capital

    ◊ The **ASSETS** are made up of everything your company owns

    ◊ The **LIABILITIES** are everything your company owes to creditors

    ◊ The **CAPITAL**, sometimes called the owners' equity, is the value of your ownership stake in your company.

- **Cash-Flow Statement** - This statement shows all the sources of your money during the accounting period and how you used it. It is very useful to you as an owner because you can determine from this statement where you have problems. Examples of cash sources listed on the statement include revenues, long-term financing, sales of non-current assets, increases in any current liability accounts and decreases in any current asset accounts. The way you used cash might include operating losses, repaying debts, purchasing equipment, or increases in any current asset account.

AUDITING

The financial audit is an important tool for all business owners. It is designed to affirm that financial statements are properly prepared in accordance with Generally Accepted Accounting Principles (GAAP). All publicly registered companies in the United States are required to conduct financial audits, and many private companies often request yearly audits. They are important to you for two reasons: lenders will probably consider the financial statements you present to them worthless unless you have had your statements audited, and it is useful to have an outside, independent agency look over your records in an unbiased way to look for gaps in your recordkeeping.

Many larger businesses have the capacity to hire an internal staff member or team to audit their records. Internal audits are created to improve company operations and they generally are not available to the public. For a beginning small business owner who may be keeping his or her own records, an external auditor is essential. A CPA can help you study the effectiveness of your financial controls.

At the end of the audit, the auditor will issue an auditor's report, which is a formal opinion based on his or her study of the firm's financial statements. Many business owners employ independent external auditors before attempting to obtain financing as well as to interest investors. Sometimes audits are even used as a tool to give the public confidence in the company.

The four major companies that conduct financial audits are: Deloitte Touche Tohmatsu Limited, Ernst & Young, KPMG, and PricewaterhouseCoopers. However, there are many smaller firms that can be used with confidence, including local CPA firms.

Marketing

The first step in developing a marketing strategy is analyzing the market. To create the situational analysis, you must research the demographics and psychographic profiles of the region you are targeting. This includes age, income, lifestyle, religion and preferred activities. Next, you must identify any competitors in the market and their current positioning strategy. Identifying open market niches or weaknesses in competitors allows you to see where you should target your market entry. After you identify a need that your business can fulfill and find out the type of development your target market wants, the next step in the process is to develop a marketing strategy. Based on market needs (price, quality and community) you can choose the aspects of your properties to advertise. You must be able to persuade the market that your property is exactly what they need.

Brand Awareness — To maximize efficiency and cost-effectiveness, it is ideal to create a recognizable slogan or logo that can be quickly identified. Since customers are bombarded by images, they must see something many times before they recognize, comprehend, and remember it. Repetition is important, but creating your brand will lead to recognition. Thus, create a certain design or memorable slogan that will incorporate your business's mission and characteristics into a marketable brand. A development can have a certain personality that the firm can use to sell it to a certain market niche.

Advertising objectives need to be created that can deliver quantitative results. For example, do not say you want "some new buyers." Instead, set a goal that you want to draw in 30 new clients, or you want a 20 percent increase in telephone inquiries. These objectives not only help you determine what and how to advertise, but also help you evaluate whether your advertising is effective. Advertising is expensive, and you need to measure your results to determine if you should continue using certain advertising media.

ADVERTISING AND MARKETING ARE NOT THE SAME THING!

An advertising strategy should incorporate various media to deliver a firm message. That message should be based on situational analysis, market analysis and desired positioning. Some of the available media for advertising are:

- Print (newspaper, magazine)
- Radio
- Television
- Billboards
- Brochures
- Direct mailings
- Surveys
- Telemarketing

Choose the medium carefully, based on visibility. For example, check how much traffic along a certain road a billboard would be on and look at the local TV station's ratings.

PRICE, POSITIONING, AND RESPONSE

Direct response advertisements (surveys, mail-in cards, anything the customer has to send back) get more action from the consumer base than any other type of advertising. The strategy should use the defining characteristics of the business and the properties being sold.

Plan a time for purchasing space in desired advertising mediums and set a date when success or failure will be re-evaluated. Based on the results, repeat the process and make necessary adjustments.

If there are better months for advertising property, use a pulsing strategy which advertises, for instance, in cycles of 4 months on, 2 months off, to minimize costs.

Marketing means locating the people who will use your project and convincing them that the space meets their needs. Marketing efforts are only considered successful if they lead to a lease or sale.

Do not be tempted to skip over promotion of your project! Many developers think that it will sell itself—but that is hardly ever true. Getting the word out to the public helps them to understand what you are doing and why it is different from other similar developments in the area.

SOME OF THE MARKETING PRODUCTS YOU CAN CREATE ARE:

- an open house for the neighborhood
- a website
- press releases
- groundbreaking
- outdoor signs
- billboards
- radio and TV advertisements

You create a marketing plan as you create the project. Marketing will vary depending on the type of development you are creating as well as whether you are looking for purchasers or tenants.

For a commercial building that you are planning to sell, you might try to offer a competitive short-term rate so that you can lease the building out more quickly. However, you might also consider longer leases that will give the development a reputation of stability before the project is sold.

Advertising

A note about naming your project: *As a new developer, what you want to promote is the project more than your own name.* You should choose the name for your project with great care, spending considerable time thinking about whether the name accurately portrays what you want it to. Is the name descriptive? Does it convey the kind of message that is consistent with your purposes? Is it a name you can be proud of? Is it too similar to other projects in the immediate area?

The purpose of advertising is to bring in visitors to the site. These may be prospective buyers, tenants, other developers, property managers, or others you have identified as people you need to pull to your site for various reasons. Advertising is a necessary expense. Normally an advertising budget should equal about 1 percent of your hard costs, but you may need to budget more depending on the nature of your project, its visibility and where the market conditions stand at the time.

Selecting a good advertising agency is like selecting a realtor; you should interview three firms, listen to recommendations from their clients, and choose based on how well their delivery suits your needs. Other developers or property managers can usually guide you toward good advertising firms.

You can hire them only to create your logo, theme, and style, or to help develop your long-range advertising plan. In addition to the traditional venues for advertising (local or neighborhood newspapers, metropolitan newspapers, radio, television, websites and signage) your ad agency may have other ideas for getting the name of your project out to the public.

HINTS FOR CREATING ADVERTISING AND BRANDING:

- **LOGO:** Your logo should be clean, bright and easily recognizable. The advertising agency will monitor the success of its use. The right logo can be carried through all of your media efforts, from signs and brochures to personal stationery.

- **BROCHURES:** These should be prepared to send to various groups with appropriate messages during the pre-marketing stage. That means you will need to prepare them about two months ahead. Since you will not know the exact pricing at that stage and since floor plans and amenities may be subject to availability, it is best to leave those items out of the brochure. Brochures can be created in many sizes, shapes and colors. If you can come up with a distinctive design, your customers are more likely to pick it up and save it.

- **WEBSITES:** A well-designed website can be a 24-hour a day, standalone advertisement for your company. The Internet is used by potential home buyers in about 75 percent of all transactions; so creating a site and then linking it to related sites like your city's site, apartment rental services, and development marketplaces can help keep your name in front of potential customers. Websites require maintenance. The customer will click past it if your data seems outdated. By using a well-updated website, you can reach more customers and provide more thorough information like floor plans and photographs.

- **SIGNS:** The use of directional signs near your site help people find your project. They are generally placed within two to five miles of your site. Using billboards, posters, bus banners or benches, and other forms of advertising signs can serve another purpose: They help to keep your name in front of the public to create a sense of familiarity.

ON-SITE ADVERTISING

The on-site displays and practices are called merchandising. The difference between advertising and merchandising is that advertising brings customers in, but merchandising is what makes them want to keep coming back. The first impression that your potential client gets from your site is critical to customer retention. So you should pay attention to the environment you have created. Carefully locate the entrance where it is easily accessible and make it attractive using modest signage and abundant landscaping. Notice the way visitors will view your entire project: is the entrance well-lit?

- Is it easy to navigate the area?

- Is the sales office easy to find and attractive?

- Are restrictive signs well-placed and small, and do they use non-offensive language?

ADVERTISING ON A $0 BUDGET

If you have just started the business and have no funds set aside for marketing, have no fear. It is still possible to advertise your properties sufficiently to get the word out. Here are just a few low- or no-cost ideas.

- **If you do not have a website, get one now**. It is possible to set up a website in only a few short hours on a low-cost hosting site. One of the easiest ways to get free advertising for your business is by blogging about it. There are free blog sites like **blogger.com** and **wordpress.com** that are easy to set up. You simply write as if you are writing in a journal, and add photographs if you like. Connecting a blog to your website is a free way to generate more traffic, and it will usually raise your rankings in the search engines. Even a blog with no website will generate interest. Blogs are indexed by search engines, and if you write regularly you will have visitors.

- **Instead of display ads, use the regular classified ads section of your local newspaper.** Run your business name and "building now" or "lots available." This is part of branding. You are getting your name out in front of the public so that they recognize it.

- **There are probably free local papers for advertising goods and services for sale.** Use those in the same way that you use the regular newspaper.

- **Find out about the morning radio shows**. Many cities offer free interviews to business owners, and they are anxious to talk about what is happening in their city.

- **Become a member of the local chamber of commerce.** Consider sitting on a committee and make contact there often.

- **Write press releases**. Every time you do something new, whether it is breaking ground, completing a project, lowering prices—write a press release and send it to all the local newspapers, radio stations and TV stations.

Worksheets

The following sections discuss worksheets you will use in figuring expenses and income. Samples of the forms mentioned are located on the companion CD-ROM. These are only samples to help you get started. You will alter them and add to them based on your personal strategies and assets/liabilities.

ESTIMATING STARTUP EXPENSES

As mentioned previously, most entrepreneurs tend to underestimate startup costs, leading to quick failure or a long-term struggle for a real estate developer, whose business depends on cash flow. To avoid the danger of running low on capital, it is best to use this startup expense sheet to estimate the costs you will incur. The sections of the sheet include:

- **EXPENSES** - The cost to get your business up and running. For each category on the worksheet, make a detailed list of everything you will need to purchase. This will include assets like heavy equipment and inventory and services like accounting, insurance and hiring architects. Be sure to use actual quotes from several vendors to get realistic numbers.

- **LEASEHOLD IMPROVEMENTS** – These are the expenses, if any, of remodeling a rented office space.

- **CONTINGENCIES** – This is a reserve account for items that come up that are not in your original expense budget.

- **WORKING CAPITAL** – This is the cash you have on hand to start the business. Eventually you will have a 12-month cash flow projection, but for now, list your best guess. After you have created your cash flow statement, return to this line and enter a more correct figure.

- **SOURCES** – These are the amounts of capital you will put in yourself, the amount that will be supplied through partners or investors and the amount you will borrow.

- **COLLATERAL** - If you are using your business plan to support a bank loan or investor request, use this section to list assets that will be used as collateral to secure the loan. Estimate the value of these items, but you should be prepared to give proof of the true values.

STARTUP EXPENSES	
Company	
SOURCES OF CAPITAL	
Owners' Investment	
Your name and percent ownership	$
Other investor	$
Other investor	$
Other investor	$
Total Investment	$
Bank Loans	
Bank 1	$
Bank 2	$
Bank 3	$
Bank 4	$
Total Bank Loans	$
Other Loans	
Source 1	$
Source 2	$
Total Other Loans	$
START-UP EXPENSES	
Buildings/Real Estate	
Purchase	$
Construction	$
Remodeling	$
Other	$
Total Buildings/Real Estate	$
Capital Equipment List	
Furniture	$
Equipment	$
Fixtures	$
Machinery	$
Other	$
Total Capital Equipment	$

STARTUP EXPENSES	
Office and Administrative Expenses	
Rental	$
Utility Deposits	$
Legal/Accounting Fees	$
Prepaid Insurance	$
Pre-opening Salaries	$
Other	$
Total Location and Administrative	$

INSTRUCTIONS FOR 12-MONTH PROFIT AND LOSS STATEMENT

Change the labels "category 1, category 2", etc., to the specific names of your categories. Enter income for each category for each month. The spreadsheet will add up total annual sales.

COST OF GOODS SOLD: COGS are expenses that are directly related to production or purchases. The land, commercial buildings or homes you buy, raw materials, and all the wages you pay to employees are included in COGS.

GROSS PROFIT: Gross Profit is Total Sales minus Total COGS.

OPERATING EXPENSES: Also called overhead, they are necessary expenses that are not directly related to construction or purchasing property. For example, office expenses (rent, utilities, telephone) and office employee salaries would go here.

NET PROFIT: Net profit is the difference in Gross Profit minus Total Operating Expenses.

INDUSTRY AVERAGES: The first column, labeled "IND. %" is for posting average cost factors for firms of your size in real estate development. Industry average data is available from builder associations, suppliers, the Chamber of Commerce, or by talking with other builders. There are also books that can be found online or through your banker that will reveal the average industry costs.

CREATING A FINANCIAL STATEMENT

Your financial statement will be useful if you are applying for loans, which at some point you almost surely will. By using this spreadsheet and updating it on a regular basis, you will easily be able to submit needed data to financial institutions or investors.

A personal financial statement is just that—a personal statement. It should show only your personally held assets and debts that are separate from the business. Do not include business assets or liabilities; they are listed on another form.

PERSONAL FINANCIAL STATEMENT	
Name	Date
ASSETS	**AMOUNT $**
Cash - checking accounts	$
Cash - savings accounts	$
Certificates of deposit	$
Securities - stocks, bonds, mutual funds	$
Notes and contracts receivable	$
Life insurance (cash surrender value)	$
Personal Property (autos, jewelry, etc.)	$
Retirement Funds	$
Real Estate (market value)	$
Other (specify)	$
Other (specify)	$
Other (specify)	$
Total Assets	$
LIABILITIES	

PERSONAL FINANCIAL STATEMENT

Current Debt (credit cards, accounts)	$
Notes Payable (describe below)	$
Taxes Payable	$
Real Estate Mortgage	$
Other Liabilities (list)	$
Other Liabilities (list)	$
Other Liabilities (list)	$
Total Liabilities	$
NET WORTH (ASSETS - LIABILITIES)	
Signature	Date

PERSONAL FINANCIAL STATEMENT DETAILS

ASSETS- DETAILS

From Whom						
	Balance Owed	Original Amount	Original Date	Monthly Payment	Maturity Date	History
	$	$		$		

Securities: stocks / bonds / mutual funds					
Name of Security	Number of Shares	Cost	Market Value	Date of Acquisition	
			$	$	
Stock in Privately Held Companies					
Company Name	Number of Shares	$ Invested	Market Value		
		$	$		

Real Estate				
Description / Location	Market Value	Amount Owing	Original Cost	Purchase Date
	$	$	$	
	$	$	$	
LIABILITIES - DETAILS				
Your Credit Card & Charge Card Debt				
Name of Card / Creditor				
	Amount Due			
	$			
Notes Payable (excluding monthly bills)				
Name of Creditor	Amount Due	Original Amount	Monthly Payment	Interest Rate	Secured by:
	$	$	$		
Mortgage / Real Estate Loans Payable				
Name of Creditor	Amount Due	Original Amount	Monthly Payment	Interest Rate	Secured by:

Preparing a 12 month Cash Flow Sheet

To create a 12-month cash flow statement, you need to look back at the 12-month profit and loss statement, and use figures you have already created. Be sure to match the category labels on both forms. You have already estimated your expenses and income, and you have determined which expenses are paid in the month they are incurred (like utilities and rents) and which have to be paid quarterly or annually (taxes and insurance).

Simply begin with the amount of cash on hand you have, and project all the receipts for the year. If the cash gets extremely low, you will have to find more cash to keep your business in operation.

All of the categories on this sheet are items that remove cash from your business, so they must all be included on your cash flow statement. Of course, if you have already started the business, you will not need the startup estimate column; if you do have a new business, this will be a great deal of the first year's expenses.

Using a cash flow projection is the best way to plan for your working capital needs. By monitoring it closely, you can avoid the problem that many successful beginning business people encounter: becoming so dangerously low on cash that they cannot keep the business afloat while waiting for money to come in. You can see a sample of a 12-Month Cash Flow on pages 260-261.

TAXES

Craig Evans said, "In your first year of operation, you have to look at the accounting end of things and be prepared. Uncle Sam's going to be looking for money, probably more than you even made that year.

"For example, let us say you have fairly significant off-site costs for your first phase, like a $2 million, plus you spend $2 million on development costs for the phase. You will have to allocate the off-site expenses across the whole project—not just the first phase.

"Otherwise, you can only take 20 percent; therefore, to the IRS, it looks like you had $1.6 million in profits! That is a huge problem as far as cash flow goes, if you do not figure out up front how to avoid it. Get an accountant if you do not know much about taxes."

The following is a sample residential lease. You can also find a copy of this sample on the companion CD-ROM.

SAMPLE RESIDENTIAL LEASE

1. PARTIES AND PREMISES:

This Lease agreement is made on_____ , 20___ , between _____, herein referred to as Landlord and _____herein referred to as Tenant.

Landlord rents to Tenant and Tenant rents from Landlord for use as a residence, an unfurnished apartment, located at _____ in the City of _____, County of _____, State of _____.

NOW, THEREFORE, for and in consideration of the covenants and obligations contained herein and other good and valuable consideration, the receipt and sufficiency of which is hereby acknowledged, the parties hereto hereby agree as follows:

2. TERM:

Landlord leases to Tenant and Tenant leases from Landlord the above described Premises together with any and all appurtenances thereto, for a term of _____ [specify number of months or years]. The initial term of this lease is to commence on____ , 20__ , and to end on , 20____, on the following terms and conditions:

3. RENT:

Tenant agrees to pay as rent for the premises a total of _____Dollars ($_____) per month, payable by check or money order, in advance on the 1st day of each month at the Landlord's address. Rent will be considered late if not received by Landlord before the 6th of the month, unless a written agreement is in effect with an alternative payment plan. Late payments will affect future tenant credit references.

4. SECURITY DEPOSIT:

On execution of this agreement, Tenant deposits with Landlord the additional sum of _____Dollars ($_____), receipt of which is acknowledged by Landlord, as security for the full and faithful performance by Tenant of this agreement. Deposit shall be refundable within 14 days from the date of surrendering the premises, provided Landlord may retain all or a portion of the security deposit for the following: nonpayment of rent; damages to property; nonpayment of utilities for which Tenant is responsible; cleaning or maintenance fees outside of normal wear and tear; expenses for removal or disposal of articles abandoned by Tenant.

5. UTILITIES:

The responsibility for payment to entities providing utilities and other services to the premises during the term of the Lease shall be as follows:

Heating:			
Electric:			
Water/Sewer:			
Trash:			

Other (Specify):			

6. HOUSEHOLD MEMBERS:

Tenant agrees that the demised premises shall be occupied solely by the following household members:

Any other people not named above may not live in the unit without the written permission of Landlord. Tenant shall not assign this Agreement, or sublet or grant any license to use the Premises or any part thereof without the prior written consent of Landlord.

7. PEACEFUL ENJOYMENT:

Tenant shall conduct himself or herself and require other persons on the premises to conduct themselves in a manner that will not disturb other tenants' or neighbors' peaceful enjoyment of the premises. Tenant will not use the building for immoral or illegal purposes. Tenant will comply with the terms of any local noise ordinances which may apply. Receipt of two (2) notices of violation of such ordinance will constitute grounds for termination of this lease.

8. PROPERTY ACCESS:

Landlord may enter the dwelling unit with the Tenant's consent, which shall not be unreasonably withheld. Landlord may also enter the dwelling unit for the following purposes between the hours of 9 a.m. and 9 p.m. on no less than 48 hours' notice: for inspection, to make repairs, alterations, or improvements, or to show the unit to prospective purchasers, mortgagees, tenants, contractors, and/or workers. Landlord may also enter the dwelling without notice if there is a reasonable belief of imminent danger to any person or property.

9. DEFAULT:

Failure to comply with any of the provisions of this Agreement or of any present or future rules and regulations prescribed by Landlord, will result in Termination of the Lease. Notice will be delivered in writing by Landlord specifying the non-compliance and indicating the intention of Landlord to terminate the Lease by reason thereof and within seven (7) days after delivery of written notice Landlord may terminate this Agreement. If Tenant fails to pay rent when due and the default continues for seven (7) days thereafter, Landlord may declare the entire balance of rent payable immediately and may exercise any and all rights and remedies available or may immediately terminate this Agreement.

110. LATE CHARGE:

If payment by Tenant is not made within five (5) days of when due, Tenant shall pay to Landlord, in addition to such payment or other charges due hereunder, a "late fee" in the amount of _____ dollars ($_____).

11. EVICTION:

Failure by the Tenant to pay rent or other charges promptly shall constitute a default and permit Landlord at its option to terminate this tenancy upon 14 days' written notice to Tenant. Failure to comply with any other term or condition of this agreement shall also constitute a default and Landlord may terminate this tenancy upon 30 days' written notice to Tenant. Upon such termination(s), all leasehold rights of Tenant shall be forfeited and Tenant agrees to surrender possession.

12. HOUSEKEEPING:

Tenants are expected to keep and maintain the premises in a clean and sanitary condition at all times. On the expiration or termination of the tenancy tenant will surrender the premises to Landlord in as good condition as when received, ordinary wear and tear and damage by the elements excepted. Tenant agrees not to deliberately destroy, damage or remove any part of the premises or its fixtures, appliances, mechanical systems or furnishings or permit any person to do so. Tenant will not remove any tree, shrubbery, vine or plant from the premises. Tenant will not store personal possessions in the common area or basement without written permission from Landlord.

13. REPAIRS AND ALTERATIONS:

Unless caused by the negligence of the Tenant, Landlord is responsible for repairs to the interior and exterior of the premises. Tenant is responsible to promptly notify Landlord of the need for repairs of which the Tenant is aware. Tenant will be responsible for any repairs caused by his/her negligence. If due to Tenant's negligence, repairs are made by Owner/Landlord/contracting party, the Tenant will immediately reimburse Landlord for all expenses.

Tenant agrees:

(a) To keep the premises as clean and sanitary as the condition permits.

(b) To remove from the dwelling unit all garbage and other waste in a clean and sanitary manner.

(c) To properly use and operate all electrical, cooking and plumbing fixtures and to keep them as clean and sanitary as their condition permits.

(e) To occupy the premises as a residential dwelling, utilizing the portions thereof for living, sleeping, cooking, or dining purposes as they were intended to be used for such occupancies.

Tenant will not make any alterations, additions, or improvements on the premises without first obtaining the written consent of Landlord. Consent to a particular alteration, addition or improvement shall not be deemed consent to future alterations, additions or improvements.

14. FIRE OR OTHER CASUALTY:

If the premises shall be destroyed by fire or other casualty, or shall be so damaged that the Landlord decides that repair is not warranted economically, then this lease shall terminate and rent for the period in which premises are not habitable will not be owed. If the premises shall become partially uninhabitable on account of fire or other casualty than a proportionate part of the rent will be abated until the premises are restored to their former condition. If heat or other utilities cease for any cause not within control of Landlord, the obligation of Tenant under the terms of this lease shall not be affected, nor shall any claim be made against the Landlord by Tenant.

15. EXPIRATION OF LEASE AND NOTICE TO MOVE:

Should Tenant remain in possession of the premises with the consent of Landlord after the natural expiration of this lease, a new tenancy from month to month shall be created between Landlord and Tenant which shall be subject to all the terms and conditions hereof.

16. SERVICE:

In the event there are two or more Tenants named herein, service of any notice by Landlord on any one of the Tenants shall be construed as effective service of notice to all Tenants residing on the premises.

17. LIABILITY:

Each Tenant signing this lease shall be jointly and severally liable to Landlord for all obligations arising under this lease.

18. ATTORNEY'S FEES:

If suit is brought by Landlord for possession of the premises for the recovery of any rent due under the provision of this agreement, or for any obligation of Tenant arising under this agreement or by law, Tenant agrees to pay Landlord all including reasonable attorney's fees.

19. TENANT'S POSSESSION:

Tenant agrees to buy Renter's Insurance in order to protect his or her belongings.

20. PARKING:

The apartment is provided to Tenant without off-street parking.

19. ALL CONDITIONS OF LEASE AGREEMENT:

This lease constitutes the entire agreement between the parties. The breach of any condition of this lease is to be considered substantial. This lease is executed in two copies, each copy to be considered an original for all purposes. This lease shall be construed according to the Laws of the State of

_____.

In witness whereof, the parties have executed this agreement at the day and year first above written.

Landlord Print   Landlord Signed

Tenant Print   Tenant Signed

Witness 1 Print   Witness 1 Signed

Witness 2 Print   Witness 2 Signed

PROFIT AND LOSS PROJECTION (12 MONTHS)

Company Name	IND %	June 15	B/A %	July 15	%	Aug 15	%	Sept 15	%	Oct 15	%	Nov 15	%	Dec 15	%	Jan 16	%	Feb 16	%	March 16	%	April 16	%	May 16	%	YEARLY	%
REVENUE																											
Category 1																											
Category 2																											
Category 3																											
Category 4																											
Category 5																											
Category 6																											
TOTAL REVENUE																											
COST OF GOODS SOLD																											
Category 1																											
Category 2																											
Category 3																											
Category 4																											
Category 5																											
Category 6																											
TOTAL COGS																											
GROSS PROFIT																											
EXPENSES																											
Salary Expenses																											
Payroll Expenses																											
Outside Services																											
Supplies (Office & Operating)																											

PROFIT AND LOSS PROJECTION (12 MONTHS)

Company Name	IND %	June 15	% BIA	July 15	%	Aug 15	%	Sept 15	%	Oct 15	%	Nov 15	%	Dec 15	%	Jan 16	%	Feb 16	%	March 16	%	April 16	%	May 16	%	YEARLY	%
Repairs & Maintenance																											
Advertising																											
Travel																											
Vehicles																											
Accounting																											
Legal Fees																											
Rent																											
Telephone																											
Utilities																											
Insurance																											
Taxes																											
Interest																											
Depreciation																											
Other (list)																											
Other (list)																											
Other (list)																											
TOTAL EXPENSES																											
NET PROFIT																											

12-MONTH CASH FLOW

Company Name

	Startup Estimate	June 15	July 15	Aug 15	Sept 15	Oct 15	Nov 15	Dec 15	Jan 16	Feb 16	Mar 16	April 16	May 16	Total Estimate
CASH ON HAND (BEGINNING OF MONTH)														
CASH RECEIPTS														
Cash Sales														
Collections from CR accounts														
Loans/other cash inj.														
TOTAL CASH RECEIPTS														
TOTAL CASH AVAILABLE (BEFORE CASH OUT)														
CASH PAID OUT														
Purchases (Merchandise)														
Purchases (Specify)														
Purchases (Specify)														
Gross wages (exact withdrawal)														
Payroll Expenses (taxes, etc.)														
Outside Services														
Supplies (office & operating)														
Repairs & maintenance														
Advertising														
Travel														
Vehicles														
Accounting														
Legal Fees														
Rent														

12-MONTH CASH FLOW

Company Name	Startup Estimate	June 15	July 15	Aug 15	Sept 15	Oct 15	Nov 15	Dec 15	Jan 16	Feb 16	Mar 16	April 16	May 16	Total Estimate
Telephone														
Utilities														
Insurance														
Taxes														
Interest														
Misc.														
Other (list)														
Other (list)														
Other (list)														
SUBTOTAL														
Loan Principal Payment														
Capital purchases (list)														
Other startup costs														
Reserve and/or escrow														
Owners Withdrawal														
TOTAL CASH PAID OUT														
CASH POSITION END OF MONTH														

ESSENTIAL OPERATING DATA

SALES VOLUME (DOLLARS)														
ACCOUNTS RECEIVABLE														

12-MONTH CASH FLOW

Company Name	Startup Estimate	June 15	July 15	Aug 15	Sept 15	Oct 15	Nov 15	Dec 15	Jan 16	Feb 16	Mar 16	April 16	May 16	Total Estimate
Telephone														
Utilities														
Insurance														
Taxes														
Interest														
Misc.														
Other (list)														
Other (list)														
Other (list)														
SUBTOTAL														
Loan Principal Payment														
Capital purchases (list)														
Other startup costs														
Reserve and/or escrow														
Owners Withdrawal														
TOTAL CASH PAID OUT														
CASH POSITION END OF MONTH														

ESSENTIAL OPERATING DATA

SALES VOLUME (DOLLARS)														
ACCOUNTS RECEIVABLE														

10

Related Real Estate Careers

If after reading this book you are not at all convinced that you would like to begin your own real estate development project, you might consider working in the field for someone else. You will gain tons of insight and experience—and you can begin making personal contacts for when you begin your career.

Many people who are interested in real estate development start out as property managers. An off-site property manager typically uses advertising or a leasing agent to secure new tenants for vacant space. He or she acts as a liaison between the property manager who is on-site and the property owner and is usually the person who keeps up with local economic conditions to establish rental rates.

A **community association manager** works in a job much like that of a property manager. The person's appointment to the position is selected by the (volunteer) association directors. The person oversees the entire property's maintenance, including that of any facilities on the property that are used by homeowners through the association. He or she might be responsible for community pools, golf courses, community centers, landscaping and parking lot maintenance. A large part of the association manager's job is to be sure homeowners comply with the community's bylaws. The person will need to be aware of governmental regulations and other legal issues that apply to the HOA or the community to be able to help ensure compliance. The person will collect monthly fees from homeowners, create the budget and financial statements, and interact with homeowners or residents every day. The person also is responsible for handling complaints and disputes that arise that affect homeowners.

A **real estate asset manager** is a property manager who also acts as the property owner's agent. He or she is the person who advises the owner or owners on acquisition, development and disposition of the real estate. He or she creates and directs long-term strategic plans as opposed to the daily property operations. A real estate asset manager will need to be aware of the financial issues as well as the area's economy, including property values, zoning, taxes, population changes, transportation availability, traffic volume, and traffic patterns. He or she oversees all the contract negotiations for the purchase, lease, or sale of the company's profit.

A **real estate broker** acts as an intermediary between buyers and sellers of real property. He or she can act as a buyer's agent or a seller's agent. Brokers are required to hold a license. A broker has spent time as a real estate agent and has passed a test that is required before he or she may hold a broker's license. Brokers are able to employ agents and may or may not own a brokerage.

Brokers may offer some or all of the following services to clients:

- Comparative market analysis (a comparison of properties to determine the value of a home)

- Facilitation of a sale or purchase

- Marketing of a property that is listed for sale

- Consulting services

- Leasing a property the client owns

- Property management services

- Facilitating a property exchange

- Preparing contracts or leases

A **Realtor**® is a real estate sales agent or a broker who is a member of NAR, the National Association of Realtors. All Realtors are either brokers or sales agents, but not all brokers and agents are Realtors. Realtors and agents are paid a commission on the properties they sell successfully. They may work for months to try to get a property to closing, only to have the deal fall through in which case they are generally not owed a commission. Realtors and real estate agents can perform many of the same services listed above that brokers perform.

People who want to act as real estate brokers or agents should realize that they will be expected to work plenty of nights and weekends. As one realtor put it, "Your time is no longer your own." Interrupted meals and family outings become the norm.

GLOSSARY

ABSORPTION RATE: An estimate, or forecast, of the expected annual sales or lease of a particular property.

ABSTRACT: A title abstract is the notes made by a title examiner based on his examination of the land records. These notes are a concise summary of the transactions affecting the property. The title agency produces a binder from the information in the abstract.

ACRE: 43,560 square feet of land.

ACKNOWLEDGMENT: A formal declaration by a person, or other legally recognized entity such as a corporation, that execution of a written instrument is the result of a free act and deed. It is made before an authorized person, such as a notary public who signs the written acknowledgment that the attached written instrument was acknowledged in his or her presence.

ADJUSTABLE-RATE MORTGAGE (ARM):   A mortgage in which the interest changes periodically, according to corresponding fluctuations in an index, usually the Consumer Price Index. There is flexibility with ARMs and if you can afford the change in rate, they can save you money.

ADMINISTRATOR: A person who is appointed by the Court to settle the estate of a person who dies without a will.

AD VALOREM TAX: A tax that is based on the value of the property being taxed, usually benefiting the city, county, or school district.

ADVERSE POSSESSION: A claim made against land titled in another person based on open, notorious, hostile possession and use of the land to the exclusion of the titled owner.

AMENITY: Tangible or intangible benefits derived from real property, like swimming pools, parks, and other attractive items.

AMORTIZATION: The periodic principal pay down of a loan. The loan payment consists of a portion to be applied to pay the accruing interest on a loan with the remainder being applied to the principal. Over time, the interest portion decreases as the loan balance decreases, and the amount applied to principal increases so that the loan is paid off (amortized) in the specified time.

AMORTIZATION SCHEDULE: A table which shows how much of each payment will be applied toward principal and how much toward interest over the life of the loan. It also shows the gradual decrease of the loan balance until it reaches zero.

ANNUAL PERCENTAGE RATE (APR): This is a value created according to a government formula intended to reflect the true annual cost of borrowing, expressed as a percentage.

APPRAISED VALUE: An opinion of a property's fair market value, based on an appraiser's knowledge, experience, and analysis of the property.

APPRECIATION: The increase in the value of a property due to changes in market conditions, inflation, or other causes.

ASSESSMENT VALUATION: The value established for property tax purposes. Those taxes are based on the amount assessed, typically the amount of tax per $100 of value. The assessment ratio is the ratio of assessed value compared to market value.

ASSIGNMENT: The transferring of your mortgage from one company or individual to another.

ASSIGNOR: The one who assigns to another person.

ASSUMABLE MORTGAGE: A mortgage that can be assumed, or taken over by the buyer when a home is sold. Usually, the borrower must "qualify" to assume the loan.

ASSUMPTION: The term applied when a buyer assumes a seller's loan and becomes personally liable for the repayment.

ATTACHMENT: Seizure of property through court process to repay a debt.

BALLOON MORTGAGE: A mortgage loan that allows for a certain term of equal payments, then requires the remaining principal balance be paid at a specific point in time. For example, you might make five years of monthly payments; then your "balloon" (the balance) is due.

BALLOON PAYMENT: The final lump-sum payment that is due at the termination of a balloon mortgage.

BILL OF SALE: A written document that transfers title to personal property.

BINDER: The written commitment of a title insurance company to insure title to the property subject to the conditions and exclusions shown on the binder. The binder is delivered to the lender and the settlement attorney.

BREAK-EVEN RATIO: The point at which income equals expenses.

BUILDING EFFICIENCY RATIO: The ratio of net leasable area to the gross leasable area.

CAPITAL: Money or property that is invested in an asset for the purpose of creating more money.

CAP RATE: The percentage at which a future flow of income converts to a present value figure.

CAVEAT EMPTOR: Buyer beware. The buyer must inspect the property and satisfy himself it is adequate for his needs. The seller is under no obligation to disclose defects but may not actively conceal a known defect or lie if asked.

CERTIFICATE OF OCCUPANCY: A document issued by local government to a developer permitting the structure to be occupied. Issuance of the certificate generally indicates the building is in compliance with public health and building codes.

CLEAR TITLE: A title that is free of liens or legal questions as to ownership of the property.

CLOSING: This word has different meanings in different states.

In some states a real estate transaction is not consider "closed" until the documents are recorded at the local recorders office. In others, the "closing" is a meeting where all of the documents are signed and money changes hands.

CLOSING COSTS: Closing costs are separated into what are called "non-recurring closing costs" and "prepaid items." Non-recurring closing costs are any items which are paid just once as a result of buying the property or obtaining a loan. "Pre-paids" are items which recur over time, such as property taxes and homeowners insurance. A lender makes an attempt to estimate the amount of non-recurring closing costs and prepaid items on the Good Faith Estimate, which they must issue to the borrower within three days of receiving a home loan application.

CLOUD ON TITLE: Any conditions revealed by a title search that adversely affect the title to real estate. Usually clouds on title cannot be removed except by deed, release, or court action.

CO-BORROWER: An additional individual who is both obligated on the loan and is on title to the property.

COLLATERAL: Something of value pledged to secure a loan. In a home loan, the property is the collateral. The borrower risks losing the property if the loan is not repaid according to the terms of the mortgage or deed of trust.

CONSTRUCTION LOAN: A short-term, interim loan for financing the cost of construction. The lender makes payments to the builder at periodic intervals as the work progresses.

CONTINGENCY: A condition that must be met before a contract is legally binding. For example, home purchasers often include a contingency that specifies that the contract is not binding until the purchaser obtains a satisfactory home inspection report from a qualified home inspector.

CONTRACT: An oral or written agreement to do or not to do a certain thing.

CONTRACT FOR DEED: A method of financing where title remains in the Seller's name until the Buyer has paid the full purchase price. A Contract for Deed will normally trigger the Due on Sale Clause in a Deed of Trust but Veterans Administration regulations specifically allow Contracts for Deed without invoking the Due on Sale Clause.

CONVENTIONAL MORTGAGE: Refers to home loans other than government loans (VA and FHA).

COMMUNITY PROPERTY: Community property is owned by a husband and wife. Each spouse has an undivided one-half interest in the property. Some states have the community property system; others do not, but instead follow the common law system. The difference is that in a community property system, each spouse has an undivided one-half interest in what the other owns or earns during the marriage, while in a common law system, each spouse owns what he or she earns.

CONVEYANCE: A conveyance is the transfer of land from one person to another. Examples of conveyances include deeds, real estate contracts, or contracts for deeds, assignments, leases, or mortgages or deeds of trust. A conveyance usually is accomplished by execution by one person of a written instrument transferring his or her interest in the real estate to another person.

COVENANT: A covenant is an agreement, contract, or promise. It may be in the affirmative such as the representation as to certain facts or the future performance of an act, or it may be in the negative such as the obligation not to do something. Affirmative covenants may be found in a deed such as the warranties of seisin, quiet enjoyment, right to convey, freedom from encumbrances and defense of title as to adverse claims. Negative covenants sometimes are referred to as restrictive covenants, written agreements or restriction on the use of land or promising certain acts. Homeowner Associations often enforce restrictive covenants governing architectural controls and maintenance responsibilities. However, land could be subject to restrictive covenants even if there is no homeowner's association.

COVENANT AGAINST ENCUMBRANCES: This covenant is an agreement, contract, or promise that there are no encumbrances against the land described in the deed or other conveyance. An encumbrance is a claim by another person against the land. Examples of encumbrances include mortgages, liens, leases, easements, or unpaid taxes.

COVENANT OF QUIET ENJOYMENT: This covenant is an agreement, contract, or promise that the grantee to a deed or other conveyance will have the land in peace and without disturbance from other persons who may have hostile claims to the land.

COVENANT OF RIGHT TO CONVEY: This covenant is an agreement, contract, or promise that the grantor has a right to transfer title to the real estate.

COVENANT OF SEISIN: This covenant is an agreement, contract, or promise that the grantor possesses equality and quantity of the land described in the deed or other conveyance.

DEED: The written legal document conveying title to a property.

DEED OF TRUST: A voluntary lien to secure a debt. Some states, like California, do not record mortgages. Instead, they record a deed of trust, which is essentially the same thing. Compare, Mortgage.

DEPRECIATION: An annual tax deduction for wear and tear and the loss of utility of a property.

DOWN PAYMENT: The part of the purchase price of a property that the buyer pays in cash and does not finance with a mortgage.

DUE ON SALE CLAUSE OR PROVISION: A clause or provision in a mortgage that allows the lender to demand repayment in full if the borrower sells the property that serves as security for the mortgage. The FNMA/FHLMC Deed of Trust also prohibits a long-term lease or a lease with an option to buy.

DUE DILIGENCE: Doing your research or homework. Due diligence refers to the care a reasonable person should take before entering into an agreement or a transaction with another party.

EARNEST MONEY DEPOSIT: A deposit made by the potential homebuyer to show serious interest in buying a house.

EASEMENT: The right to use the land of another for a specific limited purpose. These could exist for use of utility lines, driveways, and ingress and egress. Easements can be made temporary or permanent.

ENCUMBRANCE: Any lien, liability or charge against a property.

EQUITY: A homeowner's financial interest in a property. Equity is the difference between the fair market value of the property and the amount still owed on its mortgage and other liens.

EQUITY SHARING: A form of joint ownership between an owner/occupant and an owner/investor. The investor takes depreciation deductions for his share of the ownership. The occupant receives a portion of the tax write-offs for interest and taxes and a part of his monthly payment is treated as rent. The co-owners divide the profit upon sale of the property. Compare, Joint Ownership.

ESCROW: An item of value (usually money) that is deposited with a third party to be delivered upon the fulfillment of a condition. For example, the earnest money deposit is put into escrow until it is delivered to the seller upon closing the transaction.

ESCROW ACCOUNT: An escrow account collects monthly funds that will be used to pay items like mortgage insurance premiums, homeowner's insurance premiums, and property taxes.

ESCROW DISBURSEMENTS: The use of escrow funds to pay real estate taxes, hazard insurance, mortgage insurance, and other property expenses as they become due.

FAIR MARKET VALUE: The highest price that a buyer, willing but not compelled to buy, would pay, and the lowest a seller, willing but not compelled to sell, would accept.

FEE SIMPLE: The absolute total interest in real property.

FHA MORTGAGE: A mortgage that is insured by the Federal Housing Administration (FHA).

FIRST MORTGAGE: The mortgage that is in first place among any loans recorded against a property. Usually the first recorded mortgage is the first mortgage, but not always.

FIXED-RATE MORTGAGE: A mortgage in which the interest rate does not change during the entire term of the loan. This also usually means the payment will remain fixed.

FIXTURES: An item of personal property that is physically attached to real property so that it can not be removed without damage to the real property. It therefore becomes a part of the real property.

FORECLOSURE: The process by which a lender sells a property that is secured by a loan to repay the loan.

FSBO: Short for "For Sale By Owner."

GENERAL WARRANTY DEED: The Grantor warrants title against all claims.

GOVERNMENT LOAN: A mortgage insured by the Federal Housing Administration (FHA) or guaranteed by the Department of Veterans Affairs (VA) or the Rural Housing Service (RHS). Mortgages that are not government loans are called conventional loans.

HOMESTEAD DEED: A declaration filed in the land records that an individual is asserting his homestead exemption. That exemption allows one to protect up to $5,000 in assets (plus $500 per dependent) against the claims of creditors.

INDEMNIFICATION: Protection or security against damage or loss.

INGRESS AND EGRESS: Applied to Easements, meaning the right to go in and out over a piece of property but not the right to park on it.

INSURABLE TITLE: A title that can be subject to a defect or claim, which a title insurance company is willing to insure against.

JOINT TENANCY: A form of ownership or taking title to property that means each party owns the whole property and that ownership is not separate. In the event of the death of one party, the survivor owns the property in its entirety.

LENDER'S TITLE INSURANCE: A Title Insurance policy covering the lender for the loan amount. The coverage declines as the loan is paid down and when the loan is paid off, there is no further coverage.

LIEN: A claim or charge against property. Property is said to be encumbered by a lien, and the lien must be removed to clear title.

MORTGAGE INSURANCE PREMIUM (MIP):   The amount paid by a mortgagor for mortgage insurance, either to a government agency such as the Federal Housing Administration (FHA) or to a private mortgage insurance (MI) company.

MECHANIC'S LIEN: This lien is on real estate held by any person for labor, services, or materials furnished in connection with the construction or improvement upon real estate. It is often created by the statutes of a particular state.

MESNE: Intermediate; intervening; the middle between two extremes, especially of rank or time.

MORTGAGE: A mortgage is a written instrument giving an interest in real estate from one person, the mortgagor, to another person, the mortgagee, as security for a debt or performance of a duty. Depending on the laws of a particular state, a mortgage may create an actual transfer of title, or it may create a lien with the mortgagor retaining title to the property.

METES AND BOUNDS: This survey system uses natural land features, such as trees and streams, as well as neighboring landowners, along with distances to describe plots of land, instead of using lot numbers.

METROPOLITAN STATISTICAL AREA: One or more counties that have a population of at least 50,000.

MICROPOLITAN STATISTICAL AREA: An urban cluster of 10,000 – 49,999 inhabitants.

MINIPERM LOAN: A short-term loan that is meant as an interim loan between a construction loan and a permanent loan.

MIXED USE DEVELOPMENT: Can be one or several buildings; it combines several revenue producing kinds of uses. It could be mixed types of homes, or a building with retail space, office space, and perhaps living space all in one development.

MORTGAGE: A legal document that pledges a property to the lender as security for payment of a debt.

MORTGAGEE: The lender in a mortgage agreement.

MORTGAGE INSURANCE (MI): Insurance that covers the lender against some of the losses incurred as a result of a default on a home loan. Mortgage insurance is usually required in one form or another on all loans that have a loan-to-value higher than 80 percent. FHA loans and certain first-time homebuyer programs require mortgage insurance regardless of the loan-to-value.

NATIONAL HOUSING ACT OF 1968: This legislation created programs to encourage production of low income housing.

NOTE: A written promise to pay a certain sum of money at a certain time. A negotiable note starts "Pay to the order of" and is transferable by endorsement similar to a check.

OWNER'S TITLE INSURANCE: A policy of Title Insurance for the buyer insuring the full purchase price of the property. The insurance premium is paid at settlement, and the coverage continues forever.

PARTICIPATION LOAN: A mortgage in which several lenders share. The originating lender is the "lead" lender.

PASSIVE INVESTOR: Investor who wants to invest funds to earn income but does not want to pursue an active role in the operations.

PLAT: A map showing the division of a piece of land with lots, streets and, if applicable, common area.

PREPAYMENT PENALTY: An additional charge imposed by the lender for paying off a loan before the due date.

PRO FORMA: A model that is used to formulate the basis for real business documents, like cash flow and income statements.

PUD: A zoning classification for planned unit developments that include mixed uses or varied types of housing.

PURCHASE AGREEMENT: Written contract signed by the buyer and seller stating the terms and conditions under which a property will be sold.

QUITCLAIM DEED: A deed releasing whatever interest you may hold in a property but making no warranty whatsoever. It does not covenant or warrant that the grantor's interest is valid, and it does not contain any of the covenants or warranties typically found in a warranty deed.

REAL ESTATE: Real estate, sometimes called real property, is land and anything permanently attached to it, such as buildings.

REAL ESTATE CONTRACT: A contract for the purchase, sale, exchange, or conveyance of real estate between parties.

REIT: A type of ownership that provides limited liability, no tax, and liquidity. The ownership is offered in shares, much like stock.

REALTOR®: A realtor is a member of the National Association of Realtors®.

RESTRICTIVE COVENANT: A restrictive covenant is an agreement, contract, or promise by one person who agrees not to do something. If found in a deed, it is the restriction or prohibition of certain uses of the land transferred.

RIPARIAN RIGHTS: The rights to a water source by the owners whose land is adjacent to the water. These owners have rights to "reasonable use" of the water. The rights are not transferable.

SUBJECT TO: Taking title to property with a lien but not agreeing to be personally responsible for the lien. If the holder who forecloses on the lien can take the property but may not collect any money from the owner who took "subject to".

TENANTS BY THE ENTIRETY: A husband and wife own the property with the common law right of survivorship; if one dies, the other automatically inherits.

TENANT IN COMMON: Two or more persons own the property with no right of survivorship. If one dies, his interest passes to his heirs, not necessarily the co-owner. Either party, or a creditor of one, may sue to partition the property.

TITLE INSURANCE: Insurance against loss or damage as a result of defect in title ownership to a particular piece of property. Title insurance covers mistakes made during a Title Search as well as matters which could not be found or discovered in the public records such as missing heirs, mistakes, fraud and forgery.

TENANCY BY THE ENTIRETY: A tenancy by the entirety is created by a conveyance to husband and wife, whereupon each becomes seized and possessed of the entire estate, and after the death of one the survivor takes the whole.

TENANCY IN COMMON: A tenancy in common is a form of ownership of title to real estate by two or more persons in which, although they have a unity of possession, they each have separate and distinct titles. In the event that one of the tenants in common dies, his or her title passes not to the other tenant in common but to his or her estate or heirs.

TITLE: Title means ownership of real estate. Clear title means such ownership of real estate is free and clear of the claims of others. Clouded title means the ownership is marred by some claim of another person or persons, which hinders or impedes the ability of the owner of the real estate to transfer title. The title or ownership of real estate includes a right to use, enjoy, and transfer the real estate as allowed by the laws of the particular state.

WARRANTY DEED: A warranty deed is a deed that warrants good and clear title to the real estate transferred. It often includes some or all of the following: warranties including seisin, quiet enjoyment, right to convey, freedom from encumbrances, and defense of the title against all claims.

TITLE SEARCH: An examination of the public records to find facts concerning the ownership of real estate. The title search includes viewing court records to determine who truly has rights to the property.

UNDERWRITERS: Employed by mortgage lenders, underwriters recommend whether to make a loan approval based on an applicant's credit and the value of his or her loan collateral.

URBAN RENEWAL: Improving and redeveloping an area by using government action or government assistance.

USURY: Charging more than the maximum legally permitted rate of interest. There is no usury limit for loans secured by a first trust.

WRAPAROUND: The debt secured includes an existing debt already on the property. Payments made to the holder of the wraparound include payments due on the existing loan, and the holder must forward the appropriate portion of each payment to the existing noteholder. Wraparounds are typically used to avoid a Prepayment Penalty or a Due on Sale Clause.

ZONE OF TRANSITION: The neighborhoods that surround a city's central business district.

ZONING: The regulation of private land use and development by local government.

Endnotes

i   Construction Funding: The Process of Real Estate Development, Appraisal, and Finance, Third Edition, Collier and Collier, New York, New York, 2002.

ii   Peiser, Richard and Frej, Anne, Professional Real Estate Devlopment, 2nd edition, ULI 2003.

iii http://www.nahb.org/generic.aspx?sectionID=127&genericContentID=384

iv http://www.census.gov/const/www/charindex.html#multiunit

v   http://www.hud.gov/offices/cpd/affordable housing/index.cfm

vi P. 242 PRED

vii http://imaps.indygov.org/ed_portal/studies/underserved_markets.pdf

viii   P. 332 PRED

ix   United States GAO, Public-Private Partnerships: terms
     Related to Building and Facility Partnerships, April 1999.
     http://www.gao.gov/archive/1999/gg99071.pdf

x   "Does Life Imitate Art?" The New York Times Real
     Estate, December 24, 2006.

INDEX